MEDIA LITERACY

THINKING CRITICALLY ABOU

TELEVISION

Peyton Paxson

WALCH EDUCATION®

Certified Chain of Custody
Promoting Sustainable
Forest Management
www.sfiprogram.org

SGS-SFI/COC-US09/5501

1   2   3   4   5   6   7   8   9   10
ISBN 978-0-8251-6511-5
Copyright © 2002, 2009
J. Weston Walch, Publisher
40 Walch Drive • Portland, ME 04103
www.walch.com

Printed in the United States of America

Contents

Contents

Contents

Unit 7: Program Types—Reality Programming

To the Teacher

THE NATIONAL ASSOCIATION for Media Literacy Education tells us that:

Media literacy is an essential life skill for the 21st century. It is the process of applying literacy skills to media and technology messages, learning to skillfully interpret, analyze, and create messages. As communication technologies transform society, they impact our understanding of ourselves, our communities, and our diverse culture. Media literacy empowers people to be both critical thinkers and creative producers of an increasingly wide range of messages using image, language, and sound.

This revised book, the first of a series of nine books on media literacy and critical thinking, focuses on television, certainly the single most powerful communication medium in the United States for the past half-century, and a medium that is today rapidly converging with new media, including wireless communications and the Internet. The guiding principle of this book is that television can be used to teach critical thinking skills. The units in this book provide students with information about television as a communication medium, as a business, and as a source of social and cultural exchange.

The activities require students to describe this new information and apply it in varied exercises. Students will analyze and evaluate how well television serves its public. They are also provided opportunities to create hypothetical new television programming. Ultimately, this book strives to make students more informed and more discerning consumers of television.

To the Student

You are part of an audience. The main purpose of televised entertainment is to attract an audience for advertisers. Because you and almost all other Americans watch television, advertisers spend over $65 billion each year for commercial time. Advertisers rely heavily on television to get you to buy the goods and services that they are selling.

In a twice-a-year national survey called "Taking Stock with Teens," researchers at the financial services firm Piper Jaffrey have consistently found that television remains very influential among teenagers when they make purchasing decisions—second only to friends. Obviously, television broadcasters have a tremendous financial interest in delivering the teenage audience to their advertisers. They deliver this audience by creating and broadcasting programming that gets people to turn the television on and pay attention.

The television industry does not just focus on attracting an audience. It also strives to "condition" the audience, to make the audience more receptive and more responsive to advertisers' messages. Thus, the television industry tries to prevent you from doing exactly what this book asks to you to do: look critically at television and its messages. With these activities, you will examine how the television industry maintains its prominent position in American culture, and what the positive and negative effects of television are on our communities and us.

It is *not* the purpose of the author to try to convince you that all television is bad! In fact, much of television programming is entertaining, educational, and informative. There are times when all of us want to (or need to) laugh. Watching television is a very helpful way to relax. Television can bring us interesting stories, whether real or fictional, about lives and situations that are very different from our own. Television also provides important news about what is happening in our city, our country, and the world.

The purpose of the activities is to:

- present you with methods for evaluating the quality of the information that television provides us

- encourage you to investigate your relationship with television

- help you become more knowledgeable about how the television industry gets you to watch television, what messages it wants you to receive, and sometimes, what the television industry doesn't want you to know about television

- anticipate television's future role in society as communication technology continues to evolve and converge

The objectives of this unit are to help students:

- develop a historical view of television in American society

- understand the causal relationship between the commercial focus of the television industry and the types of programming available to viewers

- look beyond the entertainment television offers and consider the reality that the television industry maintains an economic agenda driven by its reliance on advertising

- understand that television constructs "reality"

- realize that television programs are laden with value messages

THIS SECTION PROVIDES students with the social, economic, and political contexts of the rise and sustained success of commercial television. There is often resistance from those who insist that material of this type over-analyzes television programming that is merely intended to entertain its audience. However, television has been, from the outset, a commercial venture supported by advertisers. The firms that own television stations cater to the needs and desires of their advertisers, delivering audiences with programming designed to attract particular groups of people.

In This Unit

Changes in Television requires students to interview older people to discover how television programming has changed over the years.

Synergies introduces a key strategy in the American entertainment industry. Students examine how television conglomerates discourage competition.

No News Is Good News? looks at the sociopolitical agendas of television conglomerates. Students confront the reality that television news is often shaped by the commercial interests of the television industry.

United States Television Abroad addresses the issue of cultural colonialism—the use of television to advance American interests in other countries. Students are placed in a situation opposite that of Americans.

Your Local Cable System examines the relationship between television program providers and government regulators. This activity requires students to learn the identities of their local cable system and the local regulating authority. Students then write a letter to the regulating authority, suggesting ways in which local cable service can be improved.

Who Has Control? requires students to examine the efforts of broadcasters to overcome the power of the clicker. Students' creativity is called on as they generate novel ways to maintain viewers' attention.

Can Television Be Avoided? asks students to confront the pervasiveness of television in American society. Students are asked to identify and evaluate reasons why some Americans avoid television.

The **Federal Communications Commission,** an agency of the United States government, issued the first television station license on July 1, 1941. This first license, and most other television licenses, were issued for commercial television stations. The government had decided from the beginning that television programming would be paid for by the sale of advertising time. World War II, which the United States was involved in from 1941 to 1945, slowed the development of television, as the nation's industries focused on the war effort rather than developing a new means of entertainment for civilian life.

When the war ended, soldiers began to return home from Europe and the Pacific by the thousands. Many of them married and began starting families, creating the famous "baby boom" of post-World War II America. Government programs helped veterans buy homes. This led many Americans to move away from inner cities to new suburban areas. American industry's switch to peace-time production after the war meant that there was a huge supply of automobiles, home appliances, and other consumer goods available for sale. The economic boom in the late 1940s and 1950s was driven in part by advertising of new consumer goods. Television, which already had proven to be a popular new entertainment medium in the early 1950s, benefited from the optimistic attitudes of the American public.

Television quickly became Americans' preferred source for entertainment and information. News seemed more interesting when one could see the moving images that newspapers and magazines could not provide. Television could also report news more quickly than most other media. Many Americans seeking entertainment turned on the television in their homes rather than going out to a theater. In 1949, only 2 percent of American households had a television set. By 1955, more than 64 percent of households had at least one television. By the mid-1960s, 93 percent of households owned a television set. Advertisers did not ignore the fact that so many Americans were watching television. Some major magazines and newspapers failed, as advertisers shifted more and more of their spending to television.

Three television networks quickly emerged and controlled most of television programming in the 1950s. These were the Columbia Broadcasting Service (CBS), the National Broadcasting Company (NBC), and the American Broadcasting Company (ABC, which had split off from NBC in 1943). These networks already dominated radio during the 1930s and 1940s. They were organized around a network and **affiliate** structure that continues today. This structure is based on the fact that most local stations (local affiliates) are owned by people or companies other than the networks. By contractual agreement, networks provide programming such as situation comedies, dramas, news shows, and sporting events to the local affiliates. (This was originally through telephone lines, now by satellite.) The networks also broadcast advertisements placed by advertisers directly with the networks. For example, the CBS affiliate in El Paso, Texas, identified by the **call letters** KDBC, broadcasts CBS shows.

Besides network programming, local stations broadcast local news and sporting events. Local stations can also broadcast movies that were first shown in theaters. Local stations also buy the right to broadcast syndicated shows. These can be older shows that were once broadcast by the networks, such as *Friends*. Syndicated shows include game shows such as *Jeopardy!* and talk shows such as *The Oprah Winfrey Show*. Local stations also run advertisements sold by the stations to local or national advertisers. These local advertisements are called "spot" advertisements.

Cable television began in 1948 in small, rural communities that had trouble receiving the transmitted signals from the television stations that were broadcasting in cities. This was either because they were too far away from the station, or because of geographic features such as mountains (this was before the use of satellite). Community Antenna Television, as it was then called, featured very large antennae. These received the broadcast signals and transmitted them to local homes through cables. Later, businesses realized that there was also a demand for cable in cities. In addition to existing channels, cable networks added "premium" programming that viewers had to pay extra for. The first premium cable channel, Home Box Office (HBO), began in 1972. Today, more than 64 million households have cable television.

Over the past few years, the broadcast and cable television industry has come to be dominated by just half a dozen companies. Those companies, and the channels they own, are:

CBS
CBS, The Movie Channel, Showtime, CSTV

General Electric
NBC, CNBC, Telemundo, Bravo, USA, SyFy, various shopping channels

News Corporation
Fox, Fox News Channel, FX, National Geographic Channel, DirecTV, FSN

Time Warner
HBO, TBS, Cartoon Network, Cinemax, TCM, CNN, CNN Headline News, TNT, The CW Television Network

Viacom
MTV, MTV2, VH1, Nickelodeon, Comedy Central, Spike, CMT, TV Land, BET

The Walt Disney Company
ABC, ESPN, ESPN2, ESPN Classic, ESPNews, Disney Channel, Lifetime, E!, A&E, The History Channel, SoapNet, The Biography Channel

Each network is allowed by the federal government to own some of its own local affiliates. The networks tend to own local stations in the nation's largest cities. Thus, GE owns WNBC in New York City, and Disney owns KABC in Los Angeles.

One other television company should be mentioned. Congress formed PBS, part of the Corporation for Public Broadcasting, in 1967 to provide for educational programming. PBS receives some sponsorship money from private companies. It also relies heavily on donations from viewers to pay for programming and other expenses.

Unlike PBS, most other television broadcast companies in the United States are in business to make a profit. Most of these companies are corporations, owned by their stockholders. Stockholders can be rich people or large companies, but they also include ordinary people. (For example, money that people save for retirement is often invested in corporations.) Corporations have a responsibility to generate a profit for their stockholders. Thus, most of the stations on television are in the business of entertaining and informing us for one purpose: to make money. The more viewers who watch a particular television channel, the more the owners of that channel can charge advertisers for advertising.

Ultimately, we pay for advertising. When we go out and buy a product we see advertised on television, part of the price we pay for that product covers the cost of advertising that product. In fact, for some breakfast cereals and soft drinks, the most expensive part of the product for the manufacturer is not the ingredients in the box or can—it's the cost of advertising the product. Advertisers spend more money to advertise on television than they do on any other medium.

Changes in Television -

ASK AN ADULT or two in their 40s (or older) how television programming has changed over the years.

Ask them to consider the following questions. Write their responses in the space provided. Use another sheet of paper, if necessary.

1. How have the types of programs changed? What types of shows that used to be on television are not seen today? What types of programs are on television today that didn't exist during the earlier years of television?

2. What do you think are some of the reasons for these changes?

3. How have the activities and attitudes of male characters changed over the years? What do you think are some of the reasons for these changes?

4. How have the activities and attitudes of female characters changed over the years? What do you think are some of the reasons for these changes?

5. How are television commercials different today from the commercials of earlier years? What do you think are some of the reasons for these changes?

Synergies -

CORPORATIONS OFTEN TRY to develop and promote synergies between the different companies they own. A **synergy** is a coordinated interaction between two or more companies, designed to create a combined effect that is greater than the results those companies could have each had on its own. (It's not as complicated as it sounds! Think about making a large bed. If two people make the bed instead of one, it should take half the time, right? But when you have the combined effect of two people making the bed, you will find it actually takes less than half the time that it takes one person. There's a synergy at work when two people make the bed instead of one.)

Companies in the television industry pursue these synergies. For example, the cable television company Cablevision owns the New York Knicks basketball team. Many of the Knicks' games are broadcast on the MSG Network, which Cablevision owns. Fans who follow a team on television will often attend games, so showing Knicks games on television will help sell tickets to Knicks games at Madison Square Garden, which is also owned by Cablevision. A guest interviewed by Conan O'Brien on NBC's *The Tonight Show* may be an actor in a new movie produced by Universal Studios, which is owned by the same company as NBC. That actor's appearance on *The Tonight Show* is basically an advertisement for the new movie. Many of the shows broadcast on the Disney Channel can be viewed as advertisements for Disney's resorts and Disney merchandise. Many of the videos shown on MySpace are from shows broadcast on Fox television. The same company, News Corporation, owns both MySpace and Fox. We call the result of a group of companies joining together to form a bigger company a **conglomerate.**

Consider the following questions. Write your response in the space provided. Use another sheet of paper, if necessary.

1. Refer to the list of television channels and their owners provided in the Television Buzz section. Now watch some television, looking out for examples of cross-promotion of different channels or companies with the same owner, other than the examples given above. List three that you observed.

2. Many television and other entertainment media are owned by just a few companies. Does this make it harder or easier to start a new television channel? Why do you think so?

3. Many television networks earn billions of dollars each year. If television is so profitable, why are there so few television companies?

No News Is Good News? -

NBC IS OWNED by General Electric (GE). GE is one of the world's largest defense contractors. GE sells billions of dollars worth of military equipment, such as airplane engines, to the U.S. military as well as the governments of other nations. GE makes high-quality products. But, despite a company's best efforts, things can occasionally go wrong. Suppose that there was a problem with a type of GE jet engine that was being used by the military. This problem could be potentially life-threatening to soldiers. It could also be expensive for American taxpayers. This situation may pose a conflict for the company. GE wants to avoid negative publicity, while its NBC subsidiary wants to report the news fully and accurately.

Consider the following questions. Write your response in the space provided. Use another sheet of paper, if necessary.

1. How do you think that NBC would handle the problem?

2. What do you think is the right way to handle the problem? Explain.

3. How do you think that one of NBC's competitors, such as CBS, might handle the problem at GE?

Activity 3: No News Is Good News? *(continued)*

The Walt Disney Company owns ABC as well as Disneyland and Walt Disney World. Millions of people visit Disney's theme parks each year. Disney works very hard to keep all of its visitors safe. Unfortunately, sometimes things can go wrong. Suppose that some people are hurt in an accident while visiting a Disney theme park.

4. What conflict do you think there could be between Disney's problem and ABC's desire to report the news fully and accurately?

5. If something really bad happened at Walt Disney World or Disneyland, how do you think ABC's news department would deal with the story?

6. After 9/11, the government briefly prohibited all non-military flights. Even after air travel was permitted again, many people were afraid to travel by air. Why would it have been in the best interest of Disney for ABC's news department to emphasize that air travel was safe?

News Corporation owns 20th Century Fox Films. It also owns several local Fox affiliates and My Network TV stations. Most television stations have entertainment reporters or movie critics. These people often review new movies. Movie reviews help us decide whether or not those movies are worth seeing.

7. Suppose 20th Century Fox released a new movie that wasn't very good. What do you think the film critic at a television station owned by News Corporation would report about the film?

8. What do you think a film critic at a television station owned by one of News Corporation's competitors would do?

United States Television Abroad ------------------

ECONOMIC AND SOCIAL conditions helped the rapid development of television in the United States in the late 1940s. As a result, the television industry grew in the United States faster than it did in most other countries. Television programming can also be very expensive to create. Because of these two factors, many other countries have come to rely on American television shows for at least part of their programming. In countries with non-English-speaking people, many of these American programs are dubbed in other languages. Foreign actors replace the English dialogue in what is called an audio voice-over.

Television has a strong presence in people's lives. It is a reflection of fashion, behaviors, and culture. Because of this, there are some concerns that the influence of American culture might negatively influence the local culture in other countries. For example, the way that American men and women dress may be considered inappropriate or even immodest in some other nations.

Some critics say that television presents unrealistic images of American life. For example, we see very few low-income characters on American television programs. Those that are seen are often not portrayed positively. This may give a false impression about American society to television viewers in other countries.

Consider the following questions. Write your response in the space provided. Use another sheet of paper, if necessary.

1. If most of the television programs that you were able to receive on your television at home were from a country other than your own, how would you feel? Explain.

2. Suppose you live in another country and watch a lot of police dramas that were created in the United States. Would you think the United States is a violent nation? Why or why not?

Imagine that you are a businessperson in a foreign country. Suppose that the television networks in your country show lots of American television programming. Suppose that they also carry lots of advertisements for American companies.

3. Would you be afraid to start a new soft drink or fruit juice brand in your country? How about a new car company? Explain your answers.

Your Local Cable System -

FROM THE BEGINNING of television, the federal government decided to regulate the medium. This is because the bandwidth for commercial television signals was limited. Even if everybody who wanted a television station could afford one, there wasn't enough room on the dial for everybody. Since there are a limited number of broadcast television channels available, only a few people or companies can own television stations. In exchange for awarding a broadcast license, the **Federal Communications Commission (FCC)** imposes restrictions on what types of things can and cannot be seen or discussed on television. For example, certain displays of violence and sexuality are specifically forbidden.

Cable television has the technical capacity to allow more channels than broadcast television. The growing popularity of cable television means that many more channels are now available than in the early days of television. However, many communities have only one cable television company serving that community. This is a monopoly—a local industry that has no direct competition. The American legal system strives to avoid monopolies and encourage competition as part of the U.S. free-market system. When monopolies do arise, government agencies carefully regulate them. As a result, both local governments and the federal government regulate cable television companies.

Consider the following questions. Write your response in the space provided. Use another sheet of paper, if necessary.

1. Find out the name of your local cable television company, and write it here:

2. Find out the name of the local government agency in charge of regulating the local cable television company, and write it here:

3. On another sheet of paper, write a letter in business-letter format to the local government agency in charge of regulating the local cable television company. In your letter, explain how the local cable company could improve its service. Consider recommendations for programming, channels offered, prices, and quality of service.

Who Has Control? -

REMOTE CONTROLS and expanding choices of channels on cable and satellite systems have led television viewers to be less faithful to a particular station or network. For example, when a program stops for a commercial break, many people are likely to change the channel. Advertisers are very important to television broadcasters' profits. Our use of remote controls to avoid commercials thus makes broadcasters very uncomfortable.

Consider the following questions. Write your response in the space provided. Use another sheet of paper, if necessary.

1. How do television broadcast companies try to keep viewers tuned to a particular channel and not change channels during commercials?

2. Watch some advertisements. How do advertisers try to keep your attention while you watch television?

3. Do you think these efforts work or not? Explain.

4. Describe a practical way that broadcasters could encourage viewers not to change the channel.

Can Television Be Avoided? - - - - - - - - - - - - - - - - - - -

IT IS ESTIMATED that about 98 percent of American homes have a television set. Nearly everyone in the United States who wants a television set has one. However, for many different reasons, some people try to avoid watching television. This avoidance can include refusing to own a television set.

Televisions are not only in people's homes. They are in restaurants, stores, barbershops and hair salons, airports, and probably in your school.

Consider the following questions. Write your response in the space provided. Use another sheet of paper, if necessary.

1. Why do you think some people who can afford a television set refuse to buy one? List three reasons.

2. Do you think any of these reasons are good ones? Why or why not?

3. Big news stories such as natural disasters, national sporting events, and international wars are difficult to avoid. If a person wanted to avoid hearing anything about such an event, could he or she do this?

4. Suppose something really embarrassing happened to you and it was shown on television. How long do you think it would take before most of your friends knew about it? How does this make you feel?

The objectives of this unit are to help students:

- understand the pervasiveness of television in American life

- recognize television's role in socializing the American public

- understand the reasons and purposes for government regulation of television

TELEVISION VIEWING AMONG teenagers is actually lower than among most other demographic groups, because of the increasing availability of activities outside of the home and the need among most teenagers to feel independent of their families, especially their parents. Students will often tell you that they watch television to "escape." It may be interesting to have them explore what they feel the need to escape from, how television helps, and whether there are other (perhaps more creative) means of escape.

This unit can be used to begin a discussion with students about where they learn their core values. A conversation about how much time they spend talking to adults each week, compared with the amount of time that they watch television, may be instructive for examining the impact television has on societal values.

In This Unit

Television in Your Household has students examine and compare the viewing habits of household members.

Your New Cable Channel allows students to be imaginative in designing a new television channel aimed at an underserved audience.

Doors, Windows, Walls . . . and Television requires an examination of the spatial arrangement of students' households. Students draw a sketch of a room in their home where a television is located. This sketch is used to draw conclusions about the importance of television in that home. Students also appraise studies that link childhood obesity to television watching.

A Vast Wasteland? features excerpts of former Federal Communications Commission Chairman Newton Minow's 1961 speech to the National Association of Broadcasters. Minow chastises broadcasters for the poor quality of television programming. Students are asked to evaluate Minow's remarks and also investigate popular tastes in television.

The Rating Game introduces the content ratings that broadcasters now display at the beginning of programs. Students evaluate the role parents and older adults should play in guiding children's television viewing.

What Makes a Good Show Good? asks students to identify the elements of a quality television program.

MOST TELEVISION CHANNELS, with the exception of PBS and pay-per-view stations, are supported by **advertising revenue.** This means that the owners of the television stations rely on money made from commercials to pay their bills and make a profit. As a result, the owners of television channels such as CBS and MTV try to put on shows that will attract the largest number of viewers possible. The price that a television channel can charge advertisers is based on several factors, including the size of the audience and the type of audience watching a program.

Several different firms, including The Nielsen Company, measure the size of the audience of specific television programs. A **Nielsen rating** measures the size of the total audience for a show, based on the number of households watching that show. Each rating point equals approximately 1.1 million households, or 1 percent of the estimated 110 million American television households. (For example, if a program had a Nielsen rating of 10, that means that 10 percent of all American households were watching that show.) A **Nielsen share** is the proportion of homes using television at one particular time that are tuned to a particular program. (For example, if 20 million households happened to be watching television one morning and a particular program had a Nielsen share of 15, that means 15 percent of those 20 million households were watching that particular show.)

Demographics and Psychographics

Not all television shows appeal to all people, nor are they meant to. For example, think about two sports shows: a football game and an ice skating show. Both males and females will watch the football game, but the majority of the audience will probably be male. Both males and females will also watch the ice skating show, but most of the audience will probably be female. Advertisers selling products that males are likely to buy, such as shaving cream, will buy commercial time during the football game. Advertisers selling products that females are likely to buy, such as cosmetics, will buy commercial time during the ice skating show.

Advertisers and television stations are very aware of the differences in shows that are likely to attract a predominately male audience or predominately female audience. In addition to gender, other differences in viewership may be based on ethnicity, age, income, or where people live (geography). These characteristics are called **demographics.** But advertisers and television stations also pay attention to other characteristics called **psychographics.** These are characteristics based on values, lifestyles, attitudes, and habits (including buying habits). For example, consider 5-year-old twins. One is a boy and the other is a girl. Which of these two children is likely to want to play with dolls, and which one is likely to want to play with trucks? Different groups of people have different television viewing habits and different buying habits. Thus, different groups of people are different **target markets** for television broadcasters as well as television advertisers.

Targeting an Audience

As opposed to the early days of television when CBS, NBC, and ABC each broadcast programs that were designed to appeal to much of the general American population, cable channels are now actively trying to

Television Buzz (continued)

identify specific types of people with specific types of interests, **narrowcasting** to them. Thus, MTV is aimed at viewers ages 12 to 18 and VH1 targets viewers 18 to 50. BET aims its programming at African Americans, Telemundo is directed toward Spanish-speaking people, Oxygen is designed to appeal to women, and Spike is directed toward men.

Studies have shown that Americans on average watch more than 28 hours of television a week. However, different groups of people watch different amounts of television. Men 55 years old and older watch an average of more than 36 hours of television a week. Women in that age group watch more than 41 hours of television per week, on average. Children younger than 12 watch as much television as teens do weekly, a little under 20 hours a week. But remember that many young kids don't get to watch much television at night, because they go to bed early.

So, although almost every home in the United States has at least one television, not all of us watch television in the same way. Television companies and their advertisers know this, and make decisions based on that information.

Television in Your Household ---------------------

CONSIDER THE FOLLOWING questions. Write your response in the space provided. Use another sheet of paper, if necessary.

Compare the viewing habits of different members of your household.

1. What types of programs do the older members of the household watch when they get to choose?

Ask them why they like the shows they watch, and write down the reasons here:

2. What types of programs do members of the household who are close to your age watch when they get to choose?

Why do they like these particular shows? Write the reasons here:

3. What types of programs do you watch when you get to choose? Why do you like these types of programs?

4. Do all members of your household watch television in the same manner, or are their TV habits different? (Meaning, do some members of the household focus completely on television, while some members do other things while the television is on, such as read, talk on the phone, or do homework?)

Your New Cable Channel -

THE AGE OF VIEWERS is very important to television broadcast companies. This is because the age of viewers is very important to advertisers. Remember, most television broadcasters rely on advertisers for income. Some age groups are attractive to advertisers, and thus are well served by television broadcast companies. Some age groups are not attractive to advertisers, and as a result, they are "underserved" by television broadcasters.

Even though teenagers do not watch as much television per week as some other age groups, teenagers are one of the most attractive groups to advertisers. Most teenagers find that there are several television networks that are trying to get teenagers to watch their programs.

Consider the following questions. Write your response in the space provided. Use another sheet of paper, if necessary.

1. Why do you think that teenagers are so attractive to advertisers, and thus attractive to television broadcasting companies? Explain.

2. Most of the people who are underserved by television are underserved because they are not very attractive to advertisers. Elderly people tend to be one such group that isn't appealing to advertisers. Why do you think that advertisers, and thus television broadcasting companies, are not attracted to viewers who are older? Explain.

3. Imagine you are an executive at a major cable television company. You have just been given the task of developing a new cable channel designed to appeal to a demographic group that is currently underserved by television programming. The challenge is to identify a group that is large enough to attract advertisers, and that also has significant enough purchasing power (or significant influence on purchasing decisions) to attract advertisers. What group would you attempt to target for your new television channel? Why?

4. What sorts of programming would you develop to appeal to this group? (Examples include comedies, dramas, sports events, news, special events, and music events.)

5. What sorts of advertisers do you think would place their commercials on your channel?

Doors, Windows, Walls . . . and Television --------

IN THE SPACE BELOW, draw a diagram of the placement of one of the televisions in your home and the other items in that room, labeling each item.

Consider the following questions. Write your response in the space provided. Use another sheet of paper, if necessary.

1. Is the furniture in your living room or family room arranged so that people can watch television easily? How does this affect other things that happen in this room?

2. How many televisions are in your home?

3. What do these facts tell you about the importance of television to your household?

Pediatricians are medical doctors who specialize in the care of children and adolescents (teenagers). A study commissioned by the American Association of Pediatrics found that about 40 percent of children between the ages of 1 and 5 had a television in their bedroom. As you can probably guess, the percentage of young people with televisions in their bedrooms goes up as people get older. Many medical groups have studied the relationship between watching lots of television and obesity, especially among young people. Some doctors have argued that young people, including teenagers, with televisions in their bedrooms are more likely to become obese than young people who do not have a television in their bedroom.

4. Why do you think some doctors believe there is a correlation between teenagers having a television in their room and teenage obesity? Explain.

5. Imagine that you are the parent of a teenager. Would you allow your child to have a television in his or her bedroom? Explain.

A Vast Wasteland? -------------------------

BELOW IS AN EXCERPT from Newton Minow's address to the National Association of Broadcasters on May 9, 1961. At the time of this speech, Newton Minow was the chairman of the **Federal Communications Commission (FCC),** the government agency that regulates television. His audience, the National Association of Broadcasters, is an organization of people who own and operate television stations in the United States. Minow's address to the broadcasters is known as the "Vast Wasteland" speech.

> When television is good, nothing—not the theater, not the magazines or newspapers—nothing is better. But when television is bad, nothing is worse. . . . I invite you to sit down in front of your television set when your station goes on the air . . . and keep your eyes glued to that set until the station signs off. I can assure you that you will observe a vast wasteland.
>
> Why is so much of television so bad? I have heard many answers: demands of your advertisers; competition for ever-higher ratings; the need always to attract a mass audience; the high cost of television programs; the insatiable appetite for programming material—these are some of them. Unquestionably, these are tough problems not susceptible to easy answers.
>
> But I am not convinced that you have tried hard enough to solve them . . . and I am not convinced that the people's taste is as low as some of you assume.
>
> Certainly I hope you will agree that ratings should have little influence where children are concerned. It used to be said that there were three great influences on a child: home, school and church. Today there is a fourth great influence, and you ladies and gentlemen control it.
>
> If parents, teachers, and ministers conducted their responsibilities by following the ratings, children would have a steady diet of ice cream, school holidays and no Sunday school. What about your responsibilities? There are some fine children's shows, but they are drowned out in the massive doses of cartoons, violence and more violence.

Consider the following questions. Write your response in the space provided. Use another sheet of paper, if necessary.

1. Minow criticizes the poor quality of most television programs. What are some of the reasons he gives for this poor quality?

2. Minow connects the poor quality of programs to the broadcasters' desire for high ratings. If a television show has high ratings, it means that many people watch that show.

   What is Minow saying about people's tastes in television shows? Do you agree with Minow? Why or why not?

3. Minow says that television has a strong influence on children, maybe nearly as strong as family, school, and religion. Do you agree with Minow? Why or why not?

4. Minow gave this speech about 50 years ago. Do you believe that the quality of television shows you watch today is different from the quality of shows that Minow describes? Why or why not?

The Rating Game- -

RESPONDING TO REQUESTS by parents' organizations and members of Congress, in January 1997, the Federal Communications Commission began requiring television broadcasters to post a rating of the content of each television program. (Don't confuse this with Nielsen ratings, which measure the number of viewers.) Some groups thought the content ratings did not give parents enough information about the content of the shows, so in October 1997, broadcasters added content advisories.

The first three ratings are for programs specifically intended for children:

TV Y **All children**

This program is designed to be appropriate for all children. Whether animated or live-action, the themes and elements in this program are specifically designed for a very young audience, including children from ages 2 to 6. This program is not expected to frighten younger children.

TV Y7 **Directed to older children**

This program is designed for children age 7 and above. It may be more appropriate for children who have acquired the developmental skills needed to distinguish between make-believe and reality. Themes and elements in this program may include mild fantasy violence or comedic violence, or may frighten children under the age of 7. Therefore, parents may wish to consider the suitability of this program for their very young children.

TV Y7 FV **Directed to older children—fantasy violence**

For those programs where fantasy violence may be more intense or more combative than other programs in this category, such programs will be designated TV-Y7-FV.

The other ratings are for programs intended for general audiences:

TV G **General audience**

Most parents would find this program suitable for all ages. Although this rating does not signify a program designed specifically for children, most parents may let younger children watch this program unattended. It contains little or no violence, no strong language, and little or no sexual dialogue or situations.

Activity 5: The Rating Game (*continued*)

TV PG — Parental guidance suggested

This program contains material that parents may find unsuitable for younger children. Many parents may want to watch it with their younger children. The theme itself may call for parental guidance and/or the program may contain one or more of the following: some suggestive dialogue (D), infrequent coarse language (L), some sexual situations (S), or moderate violence (V).

TV 14 — Parents strongly cautioned

This program contains some material that many parents would find unsuitable for children under 14 years of age. Parents are strongly urged to exercise greater care in monitoring this program and are cautioned against letting children under the age of 14 watch unattended. This program may contain one or more of the following: intensely suggestive dialogue (D), strong coarse language (L), intense sexual situations (S), or intense violence (V).

TV MA — Mature audiences only

This program is specifically designed to be viewed by adults and therefore may be unsuitable for children under 17. This program may contain one or more of the following: crude indecent language (L), explicit sexual activity (S), or graphic violence (V).

Content Advisories

V is for violence.

S is for sexual situations.

L is for coarse or crude language.

D is for suggestive dialogue (usually means talking about sex).

FV is for fantasy violence (children's programming only).

When a television program comes on the air, the appropriate letters are supposed to appear on the corner of the screen for the first 15 seconds. If the program is more than an hour long, the letters should reappear at the start of the second hour.

Consider the following questions. Write your response in the space provided. Use another sheet of paper, if necessary.

1. The First Amendment of the United States Constitution says that the government cannot unreasonably interfere with freedom of speech. Some broadcasters have complained that being forced to post these ratings and advisories violates their First Amendment right of free speech.

   Do you agree with these broadcasters? Why or why not?

2. Interview a parent—your own or somebody else's—and discuss whether he or she finds these ratings helpful. What did you discover in this conversation?

3. The content labels treat "violence" and "fantasy violence" differently. In your own words, how would you describe the difference between violence and fantasy violence?

4. Should adults take responsibility for what children watch in their home, or should they let children decide for themselves what they want to watch? Explain your thinking.

5. What sorts of things should only be shown on television later in the evening after young children have likely gone to bed? Why?

6. Do you think broadcasters should be allowed to show anything they want to show on television, and leave it to people to decide if they want to watch? Or, should the government decide what can and cannot be shown? Explain.

7. Are there sorts of things that should not be shown on television at all? Explain your answer.

8. Watch the local evening news. If you had to rate the newscast you watched according to the ratings and content advisories described, how would you rate it? Explain.

What Makes a Good Show Good? --------------

WHAT ELEMENTS ("INGREDIENTS") make a television show "good"?

Consider the following questions. Write your response in the space provided. Use another sheet of paper, if necessary.

1. What types (and combinations) of characters do you think make a show good? (good people, bad people, serious people, funny people, normal people, unusual people, etc.)

2. How about the setting? (in a city, in a suburb, in the country, in a foreign place, at work, at home, in a public place, in a private place, etc.)

3. What types of situations do you think make a show good? (funny situations, serious situations, good situations, bad situations, normal situations, unusual situations, etc.)

4. What about the pacing? (action takes place quickly, action takes place slowly, action changes pace depending on the situation, etc.)

5. Now, ask somebody else if he or she agrees or disagrees with you on each of the points above. Try to ask somebody different in age and gender. Describe the person's responses to your opinions below:

Types of characters

Setting

Situations

Pacing

Unit 2: The Public's Consumption of Television

Activity 6: What Makes a Good Show Good? (continued)

6. What differences in opinion, if any, do you think would be important to people in the television business trying to create a show that appeals to both you and that other person? Why?

7. What differences in opinion, if any, do you think would not be important for creating a show that appeals to both you and that other person? Why?

The objectives of this unit are to help students:

- recognize that television shows are highly formulaic

- understand the nature of humor

- understand that issues of ethnicity, gender, and class are often at play in situation comedies

- analyze the narrative structure of television programs

SITUATION COMEDIES provide a good medium for students to begin analyzing program types. Sitcoms are shorter than many other types of television programming, and their subject matter is generally not complex. By their very nature, sitcoms can be fun to watch and fun to analyze. Because situation comedies are highly formulaic and are organized in a traditional narrative structure, a discussion of situation comedies can be used to begin a discussion of literature. Since situation comedies often deal with contemporary social issues, they can also provide a starting point for social studies discussions.

In This Unit

The Formulas of Situation Comedies has students identify standard character types and plot devices, as well as common settings.

Television and Diversity features quotes from several minority group leaders who have complained of the lack of television roles for minority group members. Students compare their personal experiences with media depictions of different people.

Television Families and Friends examines the shift from the nuclear family in situation comedies toward non-nuclear families and families with many problems.

A New Paradigm introduces students to *All in the Family* and the effect that the socially charged show had on its audience. Students then identify social issues and taboo subjects featured on current sitcoms.

That Person Is Crazy has students identify a "crazy" character on a situation comedy, then compare and contrast how others interact with such a person on television, and how others interact with such a person in real life.

Sitcoms As Stories provides the opportunity for students to analyze the narrative structure of a situation comedy.

Most of the fictional comedy programs on television are called situation comedies, or sitcoms for short. A good way to begin thinking about situation comedies is to watch several situation comedies and ask yourself why they are funny. Nearly all situation comedies are half-hour-long programs. Subtracting the advertisements during the show, the shows are really closer to 22 minutes long.

Plot

These programs typically begin with the introduction of dramatic tension. One or two characters find themselves in a predicament, perhaps brought about through sheer chance, but often the result of the characters' own shortcomings or peculiarities. The remainder of the program is then devoted to resolving this tension. This resolution often occurs through what seems to be a nonsensical way of doing things. This is because a common ingredient of comedy is having unexpected things happen. The thing that's supposed to make a sitcom funny is the situation itself and the nonsensical attempts to resolve that situation.

Setting

Situation comedies tend to be relatively low-budget programs in terms of sets. They are usually shot in television studios rather than on location. The setting is often a home, an office, or a restaurant. Characters exit and enter the set fairly frequently. A program will typically begin with an establishing shot—the outside of the home, apartment, office building, or restaurant, followed by the activity about the plot. Many situation comedies set inside homes feature a prominent staircase, which makes it easier for characters to enter and leave the scene. The setting may seem unimportant. But thinking about the setting requires you to compare how characters act in their home, versus how they act in the workplace or somewhere else in public. Also, consider the fact that, although there are literally dozens of situation comedies being broadcast during the week, the settings and plots of these shows aren't really that different from one another.

Characters

Older situation comedies featured the "nuclear family," which included a mother, a father, and children. Most situation comedies today focus on non-nuclear families, or on a group of people who are all roughly the same age: teenagers, people in their 20s, or people in their 30s. Characters who are children are usually funny because they say things that one would not expect to hear from a child. Senior citizens are often portrayed as weird, and they will often say or do something that seems inappropriate.

The Formulas of Situation Comedies - - - - - - - - - - - -

SITUATION COMEDIES USUALLY are created according to standard formulas. A formula is a way of assembling or creating something by adding different elements (ingredients) to achieve a fairly standard result.

Watch two of the most popular sitcoms on television. (To find out which programs are the most popular, visit www.zap2it.com/tv/ratings.)

Consider the following questions. Write your response in the space provided. Use another sheet of paper, if necessary.

1. How are the shows similar or different in terms of setting?

2. How are the shows similar or different in terms of the age of the principal characters?

3. How are the shows similar or different in terms of the situations presented?

4. After considering the similarities and differences above, what standard formulas would you conclude are common to sitcoms? Why do you think sitcoms rely on such formulas?

5. From one of the programs that you watched, identify a funny situation on the show and explain why it was funny. ("Explaining" means more than describing!)

Television and Diversity -

IN THE FALL OF **1999,** the television networks introduced 26 new prime-time programs. None had a member of a minority group (including African Americans, Hispanic Americans, Native Americans, and Asian Americans) in a leading role. Many civil rights and media organizations expressed outrage.

At a national civil rights conference, the Reverend Jesse Jackson addressed the issue of race on television:

> In this type of medium, there are five different types of stereotypes that emerge. Black and brown people are projected as less important than we are, less hardworking than we are, less universal than we are, less patriotic and more violent. . . . We challenge the networks because there is simply a need for them to display our contributions in the building of America. This is the fair thing to do because we have the actors, the actresses, and the viewers. The talent is there. All that is missing is the opportunity. We challenge the industry to be more American and to include all so that no Americans can be left behind.

Civil rights leaders called for economic and political pressure on the media. The Media Action Network for Asian Americans (MANAA) told the public:

> What is . . . important . . . is the beginning of a long-term grassroots campaign to educate the community on how to be smarter and more responsible viewers: If we do not see ourselves on television and in positive ways, we will not watch those shows. We will therefore not see those commercials and not buy those products. It's time both Hollywood and the advertising community wake up to the concept that if we are not included in their programming, we will not include them in our lives.

Latino organizations called for a weeklong boycott of television in September 1999. Felix Sanchez, the president of the National Hispanic Foundation for the Arts, spoke of the importance of television programs that featured minority actors and actresses in positive roles. Sanchez pointed to *The Cosby Show,* a situation comedy that featured a professional African-American couple and their children. The program, which played on NBC from 1984 to 1992, was the highest-rated show on television from 1985 to1989. It portrayed the lives of a successful and well-adjusted African-American family, and was widely credited with helping fight some of the negative stereotypes of African Americans perpetrated by television in the past. Sanchez stated, "*The Cosby Show* did more for civil rights than any civil rights legislation. This is civil rights in the media age."

The television networks responded to the concerns of these groups. The networks promised to broadcast programs that had more diverse characters. In 2002, ABC began airing

The George Lopez Show, in which all of the main characters were Hispanic. This was the first time this had happened. However, this series ended in 2007. The cancelation of Fox's *The Bernie Mac Show* in 2006 meant that there was not a comedy program featuring an African-American main character on any of the nation's four largest networks.

Consider the following questions. Write your response in the space provided. Use another sheet of paper, if necessary.

Think of several sitcoms you have seen on television.

1. Is there diversity in the type of people portrayed? If so, who is portrayed? (white people, non-white people, gay and lesbian people, senior citizens, people with disabilities, etc.)

2. How is each type of person portrayed? Are these portrayals realistic? Are they exaggerated? Explain.

3. Are you surprised at your observations? Why or why not?

4. Are your opinions of each group based mostly on your personal experiences, or on the representations of those groups on television?

5. Which do you think would be worse—to be a member of a group that is occasionally seen on television shows, but is often not portrayed accurately, or to be a member of a group that is never seen on television at all? Explain your thinking.

Actors and actresses often perform as characters who are very different from themselves. This includes sexual orientation. Neil Patrick Harris, who plays the role of Barney Stinson on *How I Met Your Mother*, is a homosexual. However, he plays a heterosexual character on the show. Eric McCormack, who played Will on *Will & Grace*, is a heterosexual, but his character was gay.

6. Do you think it matters to most viewers if a gay actor plays a heterosexual character, or vice versa? Explain.

Although there is often a lack of minority group members among the major characters in situation comedies, there are many minority group members on crime and medical dramas, as well as on reality programs such as *American Idol*.

7. Do you think there is a reason why viewers are less likely to see minority group members in situation comedies than in other types of programs? Explain.

The Asian American Justice Center counts and evaluates the number of Asian-American characters that are shown on television programs. To see the group's latest annual report card, visit www.napalc.org/tv_diversity/.

Television Families and Friends - - - - - - - - - - - - - - - - - - -

WATCH AN EPISODE of *The Simpsons*. Think about older television shows that portray a traditional nuclear family (mother, father, and children). You may include *Malcolm in the Middle*, *The Cosby Show*, and others.

Watch a couple of episodes of the current sitcoms that feature families (for example, *Two and a Half Men* and *Hannah Montana*). These shows do not feature traditional nuclear families.

Consider the following questions. Write your response in the space provided. Use another sheet of paper, if necessary.

1. Why do you think that shows that focus on traditional nuclear families aren't as common as they used to be?

2. In older shows, such as *The Simpsons,* how are the different roles of the family members portrayed? Who's in charge of the household on these shows? How is this demonstrated?

3. Who has the most wisdom on these shows? How is this demonstrated?

4. For the first few television seasons, *The Simpsons* usually focused on Bart. Then the emphasis shifted to Homer. Why do you think this happened?

5. People often criticized some of the earliest television sitcoms of the 1950s and 1960s, such as *Leave It to Beaver* and *The Donna Reed Show,* saying that these shows were unrealistic because the show's families had lives that were too perfect. Now, some people criticize shows such as *The Simpsons,* saying that they present families that are unrealistic because they have too many problems. What do you think are some reasons for the change in how families are portrayed?

6. Think of current situation comedies that feature families (such as *Two and a Half Men* and *The Suite Life of Zack & Cody*). What different roles do different characters assume? Is someone the helper/teacher/counselor? Is someone the troublemaker? Which character or characters play other roles? Explain.

A New Paradigm -

A PARADIGM is a commonly accepted way of doing something. For example, a paradigm in television is that programs begin on either the hour or the half hour. Sometimes a paradigm changes. Just one person, one event, or one television show can often cause that change.

All in the Family was broadcast on CBS from 1971 to 1979. The show is widely syndicated. This means you should have little trouble finding it in your local television programming during the week. It is also on DVD. The show's protagonist (its main character) was Archie Bunker, played by the late actor Carroll O'Connor. Bunker was ultra-conservative in his view of the world, reacting negatively to issues involving the civil rights of women, African Americans, Hispanics, and other minority groups. The show, produced by Norman Lear, was the first situation comedy to regularly examine social and political issues in the United States. *All in the Family* was widely discussed during its day, in part because it forced Americans to examine the nature of humor. Some people found Bunker's character ridiculous, and they laughed at him. Others identified with the problems Bunker experienced in a changing world and laughed with him. Still other viewers were so offended by the program's frank discussion of highly sensitive issues that they didn't laugh at all.

Consider the following questions. Write your response in the space provided. Use another sheet of paper, if necessary.

1. Watch a few situation comedies that you enjoy, and then ask yourself, "Did I laugh *at* the characters, or *with* them?" What did you discover? Explain.

2. Do we usually laugh when a character does something smart or when a character does something dumb? What does this tell you about the nature of comedy?

3. *All in the Family* was the first sitcom to regularly discuss social issues, such as the rights of women and minority groups. Describe some (at least two) of the social issues addressed on current sitcoms.

4. One of the reasons that *All in the Family* is considered such an important program in television history is that it intentionally discussed subjects that were considered taboo, or forbidden. For example, it was the first situation comedy that discussed death. Describe some (at least two) of the taboo topics that are discussed on current sitcoms.

5. A frequent subject of comedy that is considered taboo is sex. Why are jokes about sex so common?

6. There are also many jokes about various ethnic groups. Why are these types of jokes so common?

That Person Is Crazy -----------------------------

A LARGE PART OF THE HUMOR in a situation comedy is a character responding in an uncommon way to a common situation. Some situation comedies feature characters who do this all the time. These characters are typically considered "crazy," "weird," or "zany." These types of people exist in real life. But in real life, so-called "crazy" people are often viewed as scary rather than funny. This is in part due to their tendency to react in unpredictable ways.

Consider the following questions. Write your response in the space provided. Use another sheet of paper, if necessary.

1. Identify a "zany" or "weird" character on a current sitcom.

2. List and describe three things about this character that make him or her unusual.

3. How do "normal" characters interact with this character?

4. Is that how you would interact with a real person who acted like this? Explain how you would interact.

5. Are the "normal" characters on the show usually patient or impatient with that character?

6. Are "normal" people in real life usually patient or impatient with "crazy" people?

How types of people are portrayed on television, even in fictional programs such as situation comedies, often affects how viewers see those types of people in real life.

7. Do you think that the way that mentally ill people are portrayed in situation comedies helps viewers better understand people who are mentally ill in real life? Explain.

Sitcoms As Stories --------------------------------

As DO LITERATURE AND PLAYS, situation comedies (and other types of television programs) have a **narrative structure**—they're organized to tell a story. The narrative structure of most sitcoms is usually linear. This means they have a clear beginning, middle, and end.

Consider the following questions. Write your response in the space provided. Use another sheet of paper, if necessary.

Look over the following items first and become familiar with them, then watch a television sitcom. After the show, list and describe each of the following elements of the program.

1. The exposition—establishment of the setting and characters. (Who's involved? Where are they?)

2. The problem—the situation that needs to be solved. (What's wrong?)

3. The complication—the thing or things that make it hard to solve the problem in an ordinary way. (What's getting in the way of an easy solution?)

4. The crisis—the point at which decisions have to be made, and actions have to be taken. (What are the choices here?)

5. The climax—what happens when those decisions are made and actions are taken. (What choices were made?)

6. The *denouement* (day-noo-mon—a French word that roughly translates to "unwinding")—what happens after the climax has occurred, and things return to somewhat normal. (How do things return to normal?)

The objectives of this unit are to help students:

- understand how television dramas rely on conflict to generate dramatic tension

- understand and evaluate television's heavy reliance on violence

- understand how television glamorizes certain professions

- create dramatic work of their own

A COMMON CRITICISM of television dramas is that they rely too heavily on violence. In this unit, students evaluate and employ alternate methods of conflict resolution. Students are also challenged to investigate the stereotypes perpetuated in television dramas.

As teenaged students investigate their career options, they often unknowingly rely on television portrayals of professions, particularly in law, medicine, and criminal justice, in their decision making. These portrayals are often misleading as to the nature of the profession, as well as limited in their presentation of gender roles within those professions. This unit provides exercises to help students evaluate career options more acutely.

In This Unit

Violence on Television asks students to distinguish between so-called "good" violence and "bad" violence, as well as gratuitous and purposeful violence. Students also analyze the portrayals of "good" and "bad" characters.

What Is Justice? has students develop their own definition of justice. Students are also asked to comment on the prevalence of justice as a theme in television dramas.

Television Goes to Work has students evaluate the realism of the ways different professions are represented in television dramas.

Television and the Professions looks at the effect that fictional television dramas have had on applications to medical and law schools over the past two decades. Students evaluate television dramas as sources of career information.

Gender and Work examines the depiction of gender roles on television dramas. Students are required to identify gender roles.

Your Demographic, Your Drama allows students to use their imaginations and create a dramatic show of their own with minimal violence.

WHILE SITUATION COMEDIES are usually 30 minutes in length, television dramas are typically an hour long. Older television dramas, such as *Mannix* or *Mission: Impossible,* focused on one main character or one central plot. Today, the trend is toward ensemble or repertory casting. This allows viewers to watch multiple stories involving multiple characters unfold during the course of a single program. This move away from one story to several stories within a program may be best explained by the perception that television audiences today have a much shorter attention span than did audiences 20 or 30 years ago.

Another contrast between situation comedies and dramas is that dramas are much more likely to be set in the workplace than at home. Television dramas are often seen as glamorizing certain jobs. You will easily notice that television dramas tend to focus on four types of professionals: lawyers, health professionals (such as doctors and nurses), police officers, and firefighters/emergency rescue workers. Rarely will you see lawyers preparing for a case in a law library. Still more rarely will you see police officers spending countless hours filling out the paperwork that police officers in real life have to fill out. Of course, firefighters are never shown hanging around the station house, waiting hours between alarms. The real day-to-day lives of these professionals are exaggerated on television. The creators of television dramas see this exaggeration as necessary, as they attempt to make their programs exciting to viewers.

Regardless of the occupation(s) featured, a television drama's central theme is conflict. This can include conflict within a person, conflict between a person and nature, or conflict between two or more people. Since television relies heavily on visual images, conflict within a person (a person trying to overcome something they don't like about themselves) is rarely the subject of television dramas. Conflict with nature or with other people is much more visual, and so is much more common on television.

Conflict resolution is the way in which two or more people resolve their disputes. This can be done through negotiation and compromise, or through the use of one or more types of violence. An hour-long television drama is really about 44 minutes long, when you account for the time given to advertisements during the program. Thus, the program has to create conflict and resolve that conflict very quickly. Violence is a very dramatic and very quick way of dealing with conflict. (Nothing's faster or more visual than shooting the bad guy a few times.) Physical violence provides a visual way of dealing with conflict.

Some observers try to separate **gratuitous violence** and **purposeful violence.** Gratuitous violence serves no purpose for a story's plot. It is simply included in a television show for the sake of violence itself, because many viewers are excited by displays of violence. Purposeful violence, on the other hand, is violence that does serve a role in a story's plot. For example, a heroic character may use violence to save people from a villain.

Often, it is hard to make a clear distinction between these two kinds of violence. It is also important to note that many television dramas contain verbal violence—people harassing or insulting each other. Regardless of how one categorizes violence, remember that most television dramas are fictional. This means that the creators of the program did not have to use violence—they decided to.

Violence on Television -

THE CENTER FOR MEDIA EDUCATION tells us that by the time you have completed elementary school, you will have witnessed more than 100,000 violent acts on television, including 8,000 murders. By the time you graduate from high school, these numbers double to 200,000 acts of violence and 16,000 murders.

Watch a popular police drama such as *CSI* or *Law & Order.*

Consider the following questions. Write your response in the space provided. Use another sheet of paper, if necessary.

1. What purpose does violence serve in the show? Why is violence included in the show?

2. Give an example of purposeful violence that you saw. What made it purposeful?

3. Give an example of gratuitous violence that you saw. Why was it gratuitous?

4. If you took all of the violence out of the show, what would be left? Would the show make sense without the violence? Would the show be satisfying to viewers without the violence?

5. How many characters are fearful at least part of the time during the show? Why were they fearful? Do most people in real life experience this much fear in their daily lives?

6. Police dramas have good characters and bad characters. How does the show explain how "good" characters are good?

7. Can you tell from watching the show just once which characters are good? What faults, if any, do the good characters have?

8. How does the show explain how "bad" characters are bad? What reason or reasons are given for why the bad characters are bad?

9. Can you tell from watching the show just once which characters are bad? What good qualities, if any, do the bad characters have?

10. When "bad" characters use violence, why do they do so? When "good" characters use violence, why do they do so? Explain.

11. Is there a balance of how ethnically diverse good and bad characters are portrayed? What are you feeling about the way ethnicity is used to portray good guys and bad guys? Explain.

12. What are the consequences of violence on the show? What happens to victims after they are harmed? What happens to the person who committed the act of violence?

13. What, if any, alternatives to violence are presented on the show?

What Is Justice?------------------------------

PHILOSOPHERS AND SCHOLARS have attempted for many years to develop a satisfactory definition of *justice*. Some have tried to develop a definition of *justice* as meaning something that most (but maybe not all) members of society believe is fair. For example, over the past 20 years, polls in the United States have consistently shown that the majority of Americans who were asked support the death penalty for certain crimes as just punishment for those crimes. However, there are still millions of Americans who oppose the death penalty as unjust. Obviously, then, the meaning of *justice* is something that many intelligent people will continue to disagree on. Perhaps this is why many television dramas, especially police and lawyer dramas, focus on the theme of *justice*.

Consider the following questions. Write your response in the space provided. Use another sheet of paper, if necessary.

1. How do you define *justice*?

2. Why do you think justice is such a common theme in television dramas?

3. Give an example of justice from a television show you have watched.

4. In the television dramas you watch, do the "good" characters actually achieve justice? Explain your answer.

5. Suppose that at the beginning of a television drama a villain kills three innocent people. At the end of the show, the villain is arrested, tried, convicted, and sent to prison for life (with no chance of parole). Is this justice? Explain.

6. Just as in question 5, suppose that at the beginning of a television drama a villain kills three innocent people. However, at the end of the show the villain is not arrested, but she or he is killed. Is this justice? Explain.

7. Does achieving justice always mean that a show has a happy ending? Why or why not?

8. In crime dramas on television, the program usually begins with an injustice occurring for which justice is sought over the rest of the program. In real life, does justice require that an injustice must occur first? Explain.

Television Goes to Work-----------------------

WATCH A TELEVISION DRAMA that focuses on a particular professional, such as a police officer, doctor, or lawyer.

Consider the following questions. Write your response in the space provided. Use another sheet of paper, if necessary.

1. Based on what you saw on this program, describe the work of the professional you saw.

2. After watching the program, draw conclusions about what you saw to answer the following questions:

   a. How much money do people with this type of job make in real life?

   b. What kind of education and training is required for the job?

   c. What type of personality is best suited for the job?

   d. How can people get that kind of job?

Activity 3: Television Goes to Work (continued)

3. What percentage of the program would you estimate is devoted toward showing these professionals engage in mundane paperwork, research, and preparation?

4. What percentage of the program do you estimate is devoted toward showing these professionals engaged in "action"—arguing cases in court, treating patients, chasing criminals?

5. Why do you think the program is organized according to these percentages?

6. Do you think these shows provide realistic portrayals of the workdays of these professionals? Why or why not?

Television and the Professions - - - - - - - - - - - - - - - - - -

L.A. Law, A DRAMA THAT depicted a law firm in Los Angeles, ran on NBC from 1986 to 1994. During that period, law school applications jumped from 61,300 in 1986 to a peak of 94,000 in 1991. Similarly, the medical drama *ER,* which was the most-watched television show in the mid- to late-1990s and ran until 2009, was given credit for an increase in applications to medical school during the show's peak of popularity.

Many students entering college decide to pursue criminal justice degrees in part because of the way law enforcement careers are depicted in police dramas. Recently, colleges have seen an increased interest among students in forensic sciences, largely caused by the popularity of programs that feature crime scene investigation. In fact, several colleges have created new forensic science programs because of demand from students who enjoy watching *CSI* and similar programs.

Consider the following questions. Write your response in the space provided. Use another sheet of paper, if necessary.

1. What do these facts tell us about the impact of television on our lives?

2. Do you think that television is a reliable source of information for young people who are trying to figure out what they want to do for a career? Explain.

3. Describe some reliable sources of information for young people who are trying to figure out what they want to do for a career.

During the 1990s, the number of college students seeking degrees in math, computer science, and electrical engineering declined. Recently, leaders in high-tech industries have asked television and movie producers to create more programming that features careers in that industry, hoping that such depictions will encourage young people to seek education and careers in computing.

4. If you were going to produce a television drama that featured high-tech careers, what sorts of activities would you have the characters doing on the show? What sorts of situations would you put them in? Explain.

5. Many situation comedies are set in the characters' homes. Television dramas are typically set in the characters' workplaces. Why do these two different types of programs take place in these different settings? Explain.

Gender and Work -

BECAUSE MANY TELEVISION dramas are set in the workplace, these programs give us the chance to evaluate the role gender plays in the workplace—or more accurately, the role gender plays in television shows set in the workplace. There may be a significant difference between reality and television.

First, review the questions below. Then watch two or three television dramas. Write your response to each question in the space provided. Use another sheet of paper, if necessary.

1. How many female and male characters did you count?

    Female characters:

    Male characters:

2. Of the total number of female characters and male characters, how many had important roles in the story?

    Female characters:

    Male characters:

3. How many characters seemed to be motivated by romantic interests more than career interests?

    Female characters:

    Male characters:

A role model is someone whom other people use as an example of how they want to be, or hope to be. Answer the questions that follow.

4. Did you observe any male characters on the television dramas that you watched that are suitable role models for males? Explain.

5. Did you observe any female characters on the television dramas that you watched that are suitable role models for females? Explain.

6. Did you see any female characters in traditionally male roles? Explain your answer.

7. Did you see any male characters in traditionally female roles? Explain your answer.

Your Demographic, Your Drama- - - - - - - - - - - - - - - - -

DEMOGRAPHICS ARE STATISTICS about people grouped by such information as age, gender, ethnicity, geography, and income. In this activity, we will focus on an age demographic, 12- to 19-year-olds.

Consider the following questions. Write your response in the space provided. Use another sheet of paper, if necessary.

1. Of the current teenaged characters featured on current television drama programs, which character is most like a real teenager? Why?

Imagine that you are a major executive at a television network. You are developing a new television drama that focuses on the lives of teenagers. Your new show has little or no violence to resolve conflicts between characters. You want the show to be interesting to both male and female viewers as well as to a broader audience beyond teenagers. This includes viewers such as college students, parents, and so forth.

2. What would be the setting of your show (where would it take place)? Why?

3. What types of characters would you have on your show? List and describe three.

4. What sorts of stories would you have on your show? List and describe three.

5. What kinds of visual and dramatic elements would you have on the show? (Use your imagination! What sorts of clothing would the characters wear? What sorts of music would you play?)

6. Why would people want to watch your show?

7. Which advertisers would advertise on your show? Why?

The objectives of this unit are to help students:

- understand that the presentation of news on television is formulaic

- understand that television news is mediated

- identify the entertainment devices upon which television newscasts rely

- understand how television's social and economic agendas might affect news coverage

STUDENTS OFTEN BELIEVE that television news is concerned solely with the presentation of factual information. This unit emphasizes the agenda that the television business brings to its presentation of news programming. News programming must not provoke advertisers. News programs rely heavily on entertainment devices to attract and maintain the attention of viewers. American news programs must offer a perspective that is satisfying to Americans' sense of patriotism. Ultimately, "facts" are subject to interpretation, and sometimes a full exposition of facts is not considered beneficial to the commercial interests of television broadcasters. This unit is designed to help students remain mindful of these issues.

In This Unit

The Structure of Television News has students identify and then evaluate the various devices used by television newscasters to make their programming more entertaining.

The Language of Television News requires that students evaluate the use of language in television news. Students identify words and phrases that are chosen for their entertainment value rather than for factual presentation, and substitute more factual words and phrases.

How Much Information Does Television News Give Us? has students compare and contrast the ability of television news to provide information, relative to newspapers and the Internet.

Television News and Crime has students compare crimes reported on local newscasts with actual crime rates in their community.

The Kennedy/Nixon Debates provides information about the famous 1960 debates. Students use this material to examine the role that television plays in political campaigns. Students are asked to consider the visual aspect of television and its impact on decision making by the electorate.

The Lapel Pin discusses Barack Obama's decision to stop wearing a flag lapel pin during the 2008 presidential campaign and the resulting outcry from some television news personalities. Students appraise both Obama's decision and the press's reaction to that decision.

Politicians, Public Policy, and the News has students evaluate the coverage that American politicians and political issues receive on television.

Life in the Public Eye asks students to distinguish between what personal matters in a public figure's life should be subject to public scrutiny, and which should not.

What Makes American Television News "American"? presents students with information about the press's handling of the events of September 11, 2001. Students use this information to evaluate television journalism's role in discussing important issues of national interest.

TELEVISION NEWS MUST maintain a difficult balance. It must interest us and entertain us, in order to satisfy advertisers. At the same time, television news strives to provide truthful and impartial coverage of news events.

News reporters want us to think that they are giving us "just the facts." However, have you ever wondered how, no matter what has happened (or has not happened) on any given day, the newscast is always the same length? For example, Sundays tend to be "slow" news days. Major political and business decisions, which are often important news stories, are usually not made on Sundays. Courthouses, another key source of news, are also closed on Sundays. How, then, do the television stations fill their 30- or 60-minute Sunday newscasts? Watch a Sunday evening newscast and find out!

Television news is mediated. This means that the television stations or television networks decide what is news, and what is not news. This decision is typically a business decision, based on relevance to the audience, "human interest," and other factors. If many viewers will find the story interesting, the story will be mentioned in promotional messages for the newscast that are shown occasionally for several hours before the news. These promotional messages are called "teases"—they give us just enough information to encourage us to watch the upcoming newscast.

Television stations want to deliver an audience to their advertisers. The bigger the audience is, the more money the television station makes from selling advertising. Television stations often pay professional consulting firms to conduct audience research. This research is undertaken to find out what kinds of news stories are interesting to people, and how people like the information presented to them.

Timing

During the last few years, the Internet has become a significant threat to television news ratings. For example, CNN's Headline News originally discussed its major news stories every 30 minutes. A few years ago, Headline News began discussing top stories every 15 minutes. Recently, Headline News changed again, using on-screen graphics (called a "crawl" because the words seem to crawl across the bottom of the screen) to continuously discuss top stories every couple of minutes. The crawl jumped in popularity after 9/11, because it allowed for more details to be conveyed while newscasters and analysts discussed events. Most major news networks now employ the crawl.

As the saying goes, "old news is no news." Thus, even if a news story is relatively old, the television news outlet will try to present that story as if it were still fresh, adding new details or discussing other angles to the story. Many news broadcasts will use the terms *breaking news* or *developing stories* to give a sense of urgency to their stories. This sense of urgency is the television industry's reaction to the immediacy of the Internet and other new media such as wireless telephones.

Television news also tries to avoid using only **talking heads**— people sitting behind a desk in a studio reading the news to us. This is why we see lots of on-the-scene reports. Reporters will go out in **uplink trucks** to report news somewhere other than the studio. These involve reporters standing at the site of an event, perhaps before, during, or after the event occurs. For example, a reporter may be live at the scene of a fire that had already been put out several hours earlier. Sometimes, reporters are not able to get to the event as it occurs. In cases like this, for example, a reporter may stand in front of a police station to tell us about a crime that occurred earlier. These live reports attempt to make viewers feel as if they're getting news from a witness as it occurs, rather than from a news anchorperson reporting in a studio far away from the scene.

News As Product

Some observers of television news have also commented on how television "packages" news. News broadcasts often feature dramatic music, and will use words and images on screen (**screen graphics**) to package news stories. For example, the events of September 11, 2001, led several different television channels to use the words *America Attacked* to package their coverage of the events. Television is a visual medium, and newscasters look for visual events to show on their programs. One unofficial slogan in the television news business is "If it bleeds, it leads." We often see newscasts begin with stories about violent crimes, car accidents, or other tragedies, because many viewers find the visual images of these events both shocking and interesting.

The Structure of Television News- - - - - - - - - - - - - - -

LOCAL TELEVISION NEWS CAN BE highly profitable to a television station. This is because local stations get to keep all of the money made from the advertising that runs during local newscasts (as opposed to other times, when networks sell much of the advertising). As a result, local stations compete aggressively for viewers for their news broadcasts. These stations frequently rely on highly paid consultants to help them make their news programs more attractive to viewers. Many of these consultants use similar strategies. These strategies include coaching reporters about how to act and look when they are reporting the news. With this in mind, by watching several different local newscasts, you should be able to identify some of these strategies.

Watch several local evening newscasts on different stations. Consider the following questions. Use another sheet of paper to write your responses.

1. For each newscast, write a description of each of the following:

   • the station on which the newscast airs

   • the name (brand) of the newscast (for example, "Eyewitness News")

   • the names of the anchors and reporters

   • the clothing of the news personnel

   • the gender and race of the news personnel

   • the colors and design of the news set

   • the location of each remote report (for example, in front of a courthouse)

   • the screen graphics used

   • the use of **file footage** (This is video recorded for earlier newscasts about the same or a similar subject, and may be several days to several years old. For example, a sports story broadcast during the summer about a certain basketball player may use file footage of that player taped during the previous season.)

   • use of teases

2. Now, review your notes for each of the items listed on the previous page, and write a brief summary. Include the following:

   Which of the above items are solely for entertainment purposes? Why?

   Which of the items on the previous page help viewers better understand the news? Why?

3. Write a comparison between the local news programs of two different local stations. How are they similar? How are they different? Explain.

The Language of Television News - - - - - - - - - - - - - - -

TELEVISION NEWS PEOPLE, both anchors and reporters, strive to avoid sounding as if they have a regional accent. In other words, news personnel who come from the southern United States try to avoid speaking with a Southern accent, news personnel from New England try to avoid sounding like they have a New England accent, and so forth.

News people also rely on a certain vocabulary to make their stories both easier to understand and more interesting to viewers. For example, a murder may be referred to as a "slaying," an uncommon word that has more impact than the word *murder*. If the victim of a crime or a tragedy is a small child, newscasters might refer to the victim as "Baby John Doe" or "Little Jane Doe," for example. Newscasters also rely heavily on adjectives (words that modify nouns) and adverbs (words that modify verbs) to give more impact to a story. For example, a car accident may be referred to as a "spectacular three-car pile-up." A crime might be described as "brutal" or "shocking."

Watch a 30-minute television newscast. Answer the following questions.

1. On another sheet of paper, create a chart using the categories shown below. Write down all the words and phrases that you know the meaning of, but would not expect to hear an "ordinary" person use to describe what happened. Put a check mark in the column that describes why that word or phrase would have been chosen.

Words and phrases	More emotional than ordinary words	Words that provide a visual image	Easier to understand than commonly used word(s)	Buzzword

2. Now create a new chart. For each word or phrase you've listed, provide another word or phrase that presents the facts without the "drama."

Word or phrase used	Your substitute

How Much Information Does Television News Give Us?- -

WATCH YOUR LOCAL EVENING NEWS. Pick out a story or two about a major news item. After that news item has concluded, write down everything the television news told you about that story. Then compare your notes with a newspaper article (in that day's or the next day's newspaper) on the same news item. Write your response in the space provided. Use another sheet of paper, if necessary.

1. What additional information, if any, did the newspaper article provide?

2. Do you think that the television news story left out anything important? Why or why not?

3. Which did you find more interesting, the television report or the newspaper article? Why?

Most local television stations now maintain a Web site. Visit the Web site of the television station on which you watched the local news for this activity. Compare your notes on the news story that you analyzed for the questions above with the information presented on the site.

Activity 3: How Much Information Does Television News Give Us? (continued)

4. Which source of information presented the story best, in your opinion: the television news, the newspaper, or the Internet? Explain your answer.

5. Which source of information presented the story the least satisfactorily, in your opinion: the television news, the newspaper, or the Internet? Explain your answer.

6. Who decides what is "news" and what is not "news"? Explain.

7. What sorts of things do you think go into the decision about what is worth reporting and what is not worth reporting? Explain.

Television News and Crime -

THE MOST COMPREHENSIVE STUDY of television violence ever conducted was carried out by the University of California, Santa Barbara, and reported in 1998. Researchers sampled 2,500 hours of television programming in 1994, 1995, and 1996. At the time, they found that 57 percent of television programs contain some violence, and that perpetrators of violence go unpunished 73 percent of the time. More recent research shows this trend hasn't changed much.

According to the United States Bureau of Justice Statistics, the rate of violent crimes (murder, rape, robbery, and assault) has declined steadily since 1994, reaching the lowest level ever recorded in 2005. Property crimes, such as burglary, theft, and motor vehicle theft, have also declined over the past 20 years. Despite these facts, many Americans believe that crime is steadily increasing, and many Americans feel increasingly threatened by crime.

Watch the local evening news each evening for a week. Consider the following questions. Write your response in the space provided. Use another sheet of paper, if necessary.

1. How many crime stories (about both local crimes and crimes in other parts of the nation and other parts of the world) were broadcast each evening?

2. Based on what you see, try to guess what the average number of homicides (people killed by other people) is in your community each year.

3. Now find out what the actual rate is (your school librarian can help). What is it?

4. Based on the comparison between homicides depicted on televised news and the actual number of homicides occurring in your community, do you think that the television stations make people more fearful or less fearful, or have no effect on fear? Explain.

The Kennedy/Nixon Debates --------------------

THE FIRST TELEVISED DEBATE between two candidates for president of the United States was broadcast live from Chicago on September 26, 1960, the first of four presidential debates broadcast that fall. John F. Kennedy, a U.S. senator from Massachusetts, was the Democratic candidate for president that year. Vice President Richard M. Nixon was the Republican candidate. Not only was the debate itself a historic event, but so was the new way politicians used television to get their message to the American public. Most observers agreed that John Kennedy was more **telegenic** (looked better on television) than Richard Nixon. Nixon had recently been hospitalized for a leg injury, and he appeared pale and tired, perspired heavily, and wore clothes that didn't fit well because he had lost weight while in the hospital. Kennedy, on the other hand, was younger, had a flattering suntan and a thick head of hair, and seemed much more comfortable in front of the camera. Since television is a visual medium, these details, generally ignored before in American politics, now became seen as important to winning elections. The presidential election in November was such a narrow victory for Kennedy that many commentators credited the four televised debates as the difference in the presidential campaigns.

Consider the following questions. Write your response in the space provided. Use another sheet of paper, if necessary.

1. The first televised debate between Kennedy and Nixon on September 26, 1960, drew the largest single audience in television history to that point. Why do you think that was so? What do you think that said about the power of television at that time in history?

Activity 5: The Kennedy/Nixon Debates (*continued*)

2. Results of surveys of people who listened to the first Kennedy/Nixon debate on the radio found that these listeners tended to believe that Nixon had won the debate. Surveys of those who watched the same debate on television found that viewers tended to believe that Kennedy had won. What do you think is a good explanation for the different results of these surveys?

3. How important should the appearance of a politician be? Why?

4. Interview an adult who votes regularly about where she or he gets information about political candidates. Ask the following questions:

   • What percentage of your information about politicians comes from television?

   • Is there any information transmitted by a political candidate on television that you think cannot be suitably transmitted by other media such as the newspaper or radio? Explain.

   • Is there information that is best transmitted by a political candidate in a medium other than television? Explain.

The Lapel Pin -

DURING THE 2008 U.S. PRESIDENTIAL CAMPAIGN, Democratic candidate Barack Obama decided to stop wearing an American flag pin on the lapel of his suits. Obama said that the pin had become a substitute for "true patriotism" after 9/11. Several television news personalities criticized Barack Obama for his decision. After receiving this criticism, Obama decided to begin wearing the flag pin again.

Consider the following questions. Write your response in the space provided. Use another sheet of paper, if necessary.

1. Why do you think some television news personalities criticized Obama? Explain.

2. Do you agree with this criticism? Explain.

3. Most of the reporters who criticized Obama were not wearing flag lapel pins themselves when they pointed out that Obama was not wearing one. Do you think the reporters were being hypocritical?

4. Do you think there are different standards for politicians and for news personalities? Should there be? Explain.

Politicians, Public Policy, and the News - - - - - - - - - - -

COMEDY CENTRAL's *The Daily Show with Jon Stewart* calls itself "the most trusted name in fake news." Nevertheless, many young Americans cite *The Daily Show* as a source of information and news about American politics and politicians. In fact, a study in 2008 by the Pew Research Center for the People & the Press found that more young adults rely on *The Daily Show* for political information than they do on television news. As a program appearing on Comedy Central, the purpose of *The Daily Show* is to be funny. Stewart's comedy usually arises from making fun of political leaders. People expect television news, at both the local and the national level, to tell us about the actions of political leaders without making fun of them.

Consider the following questions. Write your response in the space provided. Use another sheet of paper, if necessary.

1. How are American political leaders—mayors, legislators, governors, the president of the United States—depicted on the local and national televised news?

2. Do you think television news portrays these leaders respectfully? Explain.

3. Do you think foreign political leaders are treated with less respect than American politicians, more respect, or about the same? Explain.

One source of debate regarding television's coverage of politics is how much information a politician should give. If he or she provides a lengthy explanation of his or her opinions or strategies on a political matter, the politician is accused of being "too wordy" and "boring." If he or she gives a brief answer, the politician is accused of providing only a "sound bite." A sound bite is usually only a sentence or two at the most. Unfortunately, television news reports often focus on sound bites, so many politicians provide little more than sound bites, hoping to get some news coverage.

4. Do you think that most television viewers would watch a news program that broadcast politicians' entire speeches? Explain.

5. Why do you think sound bites are so commonly used on television news? Explain.

6. Do you think sound bites help inform viewers about political leaders and current political situations? Explain.

Life in the Public Eye -

NOBODY IS FORCED TO ENTER POLITICS or the entertainment business. Those who do so, do so willingly. Yet it has been said that many talented entertainers and qualified politicians change their careers because of the tremendous degree of public scrutiny. Talented people may never be discovered because they don't want the exposure to the public. Qualified individuals refuse to run for political office altogether because of this scrutiny. Many Americans blur the line between a celebrity's public persona and private life. Most Americans believe that voters in a democracy are entitled to know important facts about the personal lives of their political leaders. The question is, what is news? What is an important fact?

Consider the following questions. Write your response in the space provided. Use another sheet of paper, if necessary.

1. Is a public figure's romantic relationship the public's business? Why might it be? Why wouldn't it be? Explain.

2. If a politician is heavily in debt and is having trouble managing personal financial matters, do you feel that is the public's business? Explain.

3. If a politician has or used to have a drinking or drug problem, do you feel that is the public's business? Explain.

4. If a celebrity has or used to have a drinking or drug problem, do you feel that is the public's business? Explain.

5. If a close relative of a public figure (for example, the politician's brother or mother) was in trouble with the law, do you feel that is the public's business? Explain.

6. Why do television news programs give us so much information about celebrities' and politicians' personal lives?

7. Create a chart showing a general set of rules for what sorts of issues involving public figures are our business, and what sorts of issues are not.

Our business	Not our business

What Makes American Television News "American"?

SOON AFTER THE ATTACKS on New York City and Washington, D.C., on September 11, 2001, the British-owned news service Reuters told its reporters that it should not refer to those events as acts of "terrorism." Reuters stated:

> As part of a policy to avoid the use of emotive words, we do not use terms like "terrorist" and "freedom fighter" unless they are in a direct quote or are otherwise attributable to a third party. We do not characterize the subjects of news stories but instead report their actions, identity and background so that readers can make their own decisions based on the facts.

Stephen Jukes, Reuter's global head of news, explained in an interview, "We're trying to treat everyone on a level playing field, however tragic it's been and however awful and cataclysmic for the American people and people around the world." Jukes told his interviewer, "We don't want to jeopardize the safety of our staff. Our people are on the front lines, in Gaza, the West Bank and Afghanistan. The minute we seem to be siding with one side or another, they're in danger.

"We're there to tell the story," Jukes said. "We're not there to evaluate the moral case."

Bill Wheatley, a news executive at American-owned NBC, disagreed with the decision by Reuters: "A group of people commandeered airliners and used them as guided missiles against thousands of people. If that doesn't fit the definition of terrorism, what does?"

Atlanta-based CNN ran this announcement on its Web site in October 2001:

> There have been false reports that CNN has not used the word "terrorist" to refer to those who attacked the World Trade Center and Pentagon. In fact, CNN has consistently and repeatedly referred to the attackers and hijackers as terrorists, and it will continue to do so.

A few weeks after the September 11 attacks, Osama bin Laden released a videotaped message to the American people. Condoleezza Rice, then the U.S. national security advisor, contacted the television networks soon after the video was released and asked the networks to be careful about showing the video on television. The government was concerned that the video might contain hidden messages to bin Laden's followers. As White House Press Secretary Ari Fleischer explained it, Rice called the networks "to raise their awareness about national security concerns with airing prerecorded, pretaped messages from Osama bin Laden that could be a signal to terrorists to incite attacks.

"At best, Osama bin Laden's messages are propaganda, calling on people to kill Americans," Fleischer told reporters. "At worst, he could be issuing orders to his followers to initiate such attacks."

Activity 9: What Makes American Television News "American"? (continued)

Most of the news media, including the television news media, strive to be objective—to limit their reporting to the facts only, free from news reporters' personal opinions. At the same time, the news media are very aware of the fact that they have an audience they want to reach. To reach that audience, the news media have to appeal to that audience.

Consider the following questions. Write your response in the space provided. Use another sheet of paper, if necessary.

1. List and describe the responsibilities television news reporters have to the public.

2. How might the responsibilities that the news media have to the American people sometimes conflict with the responsibilities that the news media have to the United States government?

3. Should television news reports broadcast in the United States about the relationship between the United States and other countries always be favorable to the United States? Why or why not?

Activity 9: What Makes American Television News "American"?
(continued)

4. Should television news reports explain the viewpoints of both the United States and the political enemies of the United States in a particular situation, or just the viewpoints of the United States? Explain your answer.

5. Suppose an important American political leader tells a lie during a press conference shown on television. Several of the news reporters who are at the press conference know that this statement is a lie. However, those reporters are worried that exposing the lie will actually help the political enemies of the United States. What would you do if you were one of the reporters in this situation? Explain your answer.

The objectives of this unit are to help students:

- understand the symbiotic relationship between sports leagues and television

- understand the different demographic appeal of different types of sports and the resulting effects on advertising

- understand the dramatic elements that underlie scripted professional wrestling

- understand the role televised sports play in American culture

- understand the commercial and cultural imperatives that confer athletes with celebrity status

SOME STUDENTS MAY PROTEST that they dislike sports. These students can often provide excellent insights into America's fascination with sports, as they have the distance from this fascination that provides them with perspective. For students who are rabid (or at least interested) sports fans, it may prove challenging to step back and try to gain this perspective. This unit is designed to accommodate both groups of students.

In This Unit

What's Wrong with Hockey on Television? has students examine the visual requirements of television and the demographics of hockey fans.

NASCAR's Popularity asks students to examine the relationship between sports and commercialism.

Pro Wrestling: Good versus Evil has students evaluate the morality play that takes place in the scripted sport.

Golf versus Wrestling involves evaluation of the different demographics of the audiences for televised sports.

The Super Bowl discusses the social and national impulse to gather around a common event.

A Word from Our Sponsor asks students to evaluate the degree of commercialism associated with broadcasts of sporting events.

Athletes: The Rich and the Famous invites students to examine the personality cult that surrounds athletes.

COMMERCIAL TELEVISION AS WE KNOW IT became popular after World War II. Much of the U.S. efforts to develop technology during the war were directed toward the defense industry. After the war, many of the technical advances that helped the military during the war were converted to more peaceful uses. Advances in telecommunications during the war allowed consumers to gain access to television soon after the war ended.

The 1950s are often considered the "glory days" of television. Movie theater attendance declined as more and more Americans decided to stay home and watch television rather than go out to the movies. Because there was relatively little television programming available during the early days of television, you may hear stories from older Americans about how they would sometimes simply sit and stare at test patterns on television, waiting for broadcasting to resume.

Technology and Sports

Technological advances during World War II also meant tremendous improvements in passenger airline travel after the war. The ability to travel quickly across the country meant that professional sports leagues, which had previously had most of their teams east of the Mississippi River, could expand to cities in California and other western states. The movement toward truly national sports leagues was attractive to television broadcasting companies, which were looking for more programming and national audiences that would attract national advertisers. In 1946, the Cleveland Rams football team moved to Los Angeles. In 1958, the Brooklyn Dodgers and New York Giants baseball teams moved, respectively, to Los Angeles and San Francisco. The Minneapolis Lakers basketball team moved to Los Angeles two years later.

Sports on TV: A Slam Dunk

Sports are attractive to television broadcasters because people in general like sports and they like to watch sports on television. Sports also provide easy programming for television; all the television companies have to do is broadcast games that were already going to take place anyway, rather than write and produce programs of their own.

The sports leagues are also attracted to television. In addition to selling tickets in the arena and stadium, the leagues can charge television companies for the right to broadcast their games. The effort by sports leagues to gain television audiences, and thus television revenue, means that sports leagues are occasionally willing to change some of the rules of their games in order to accommodate the television industry's concerns. (Think of something as simple as the "television time-out" that is common during most sports broadcasts.) In general, television audiences tend to want games that move quickly, with lots of scoring. In fact, the lack of high-scoring games is pointed to as one reason why professional soccer has had little success on American television.

The relationship between sports (both professional and amateur sports) and television is extremely important to sports leagues and to television broadcasters. Certainly, sports as we know them today could not exist without television.

What's Wrong with Hockey on Television? --------

AMONG NATIONALLY TELEVISED SPORTS, professional hockey ratings have historically been very low. Part of the reason for this may have been the limited national appeal; hockey enthusiasts are traditionally in the northeast United States and in Canada. However, with the expansion of the National Hockey League (NHL) into the southern United States (there are two teams in Florida, two teams in southern California, and teams in Phoenix, Dallas, Nashville, Atlanta, and North Carolina), the national appeal of hockey has increased. Average attendance at NHL games is actually higher than attendance at National Basketball Association games. Despite the NHL's geographic expansion and its loyal fans, professional hockey continues to suffer from poor television ratings. Some observers point out that hockey is not **telegenic**—that hockey is not visually appealing on television.

Watch at least 15 minutes of a professional hockey game, and then answer the following questions. Write your response in the space provided. Use another sheet of paper, if necessary.

1. List and describe at least three reasons why you think professional hockey generally does not receive very good television ratings.

2. Imagine that you are an executive either with the NHL or with a television network that broadcasts NHL games. List three suggestions for how hockey could make itself more popular to television audiences, providing your reasoning for each suggestion.

3. In areas where hockey has been a long-time tradition, the sport's fans have been primarily white working-class males. In recent years, professional hockey's fan base has expanded and diversified. Newer NHL teams attract more fans than the older teams. Fans of newer teams include more women, more non-whites, and all economic classes. How do you think the television networks feel about this trend? Explain.

4. Why do you think the sport's fan base has seen this shift in demographics?

NASCAR's Popularity -

PROFESSIONAL STOCK CAR RACING BEGAN in the 1920s as the result of bootleggers (makers of illegal alcoholic beverages) using fast cars to outrun law enforcement during Prohibition, when manufacturing alcoholic beverages was against the law in the United States. Owners of these tricked-out cars began to race each other, sometimes for money, and this tradition continued after Prohibition ended in the early 1930s. In the early 1970s, the advertising of tobacco products was banned on television. Tobacco companies saw car racing as an attractive alternative. By providing sponsorship money for drivers, tobacco companies could have their names placed prominently on the race cars, where the tobacco brand name could be clearly seen by fans attending the race, and by others watching the race on television. One series of races was named the Winston Cup (after a cigarette brand) until 2003. Most tobacco firms are no longer involved in advertising in car racing today. However, many alcoholic beverage firms, especially brewers, are still associated with car racing.

In the 1980s, cable sports networks such as ESPN went on the air and were looking for various types of sporting events that would fill their need for 24-hour sports programming. Various forms of automobile racing help these cable sports networks fill their broadcasting schedules. Today, the leading stock car racing organization, NASCAR (the National Association for Stock Car Auto Racing), has seen a steady growth in television viewership among young adult males.

Consider the following questions. Write your response in the space provided. Use another sheet of paper, if necessary.

1. One explanation for the surging popularity of NASCAR racing is that fans imagine themselves being behind the steering wheels of the race cars as they careen around the track. Why do you think people might like feeling this way?

2. Watch a few minutes of a NASCAR race. Why do you think NASCAR is so popular among advertisers? Explain.

3. Some people say that the best part of a car race is when drivers crash. Why do you think they say this? Do you agree? Why or why not?

4. The former Winston Cup series of NASCAR races is now called the Sprint Cup. Do some research on the Internet and find out why NASCAR made this name change. Describe what you find.

5. Do you think it was a good idea for NASCAR to make this name change? Explain.

6. NASCAR driver Kurt Busch races a car sponsored by Miller Lite Beer. Budweiser sponsors driver Kasey Kahne. Clint Bowyer drives a car sponsored in part by winemaker Childress Vineyards. Robby Gordon drives a Dodge sponsored by Jim Beam, which makes bourbon.

    Some people are concerned that advertisements for various brands of alcoholic beverages appear on NASCAR race cars. Why do you think these people are concerned? Explain.

7. Imagine that you are one of the top executives at NASCAR. Would you continue to allow alcoholic beverage makers to have their names on the cars and clothing of NASCAR drivers? Explain.

Pro Wrestling: Good versus Evil - - - - - - - - - - - - - - - - -

PROFESSIONAL WRESTLING, OR PRO WRESTLING, has been around as a form of entertainment since the 1800s. The matches are prearranged. While the wrestlers appear to be combative, most of the actions they take are heavily scripted and designed for dramatic effect. Most wrestling matches even have a backstory, and the wrestlers themselves are playing characters in a storyline.

Watch some professional wrestling, such as World Wrestling Entertainment (WWE).

Consider the following questions. Write your response in the space provided. Use another sheet of paper, if necessary.

1. What makes the good guys "good"? What makes the bad guys "bad"? Explain.

2. Why is it so important in professional wrestling to have some "good" guys and some "bad" guys?

3. Is it easier to decide who is "good" and "bad" in professional wrestling than it is in real life? Explain.

4. Each professional wrestler seems to have a clearly defined personality. (If you're uncertain what those personalities are, read some of the wrestlers' profiles at wwe.com.) Why do you think that WWE tries to define each wrestler's personality?

5. How is "otherness" (people of different ethnicities, people from different countries, people of different cultures) represented among professional wrestlers? Give examples.

6. How are women portrayed in wrestling? Why do you think they are portrayed this way?

Golf versus Wrestling ----------------------------

WATCH AT LEAST 15 MINUTES of a televised golf tournament and at least 15 minutes of a professional wrestling program.

Consider the following questions. Write your response in the space provided. Use another sheet of paper, if necessary.

1. How do the television announcers behave during the golf tournament? How do the announcers behave during the wrestling program? How are they alike? How are they different? Explain.

2. What types of products are advertised during a golf tournament? What types of products are advertised during professional wrestling? Are there similarities or differences? What are they? Explain.

3. Professional wrestling programs such as WWE's Raw and SmackDown often have twice as many viewers as a televised golf tournament. Why, then, do advertisers place their advertisements on golf programs?

The Super Bowl -

THE SUPER BOWL normally receives some of the highest ratings of all television programs. Generally, about 158 million people, or over half of the U.S. population of 304 million people, will watch all or at least part of the Super Bowl each year. This is true even when the teams playing are not the favorite teams of most of the viewers watching. In addition, many people who watch the Super Bowl don't really even like football, no matter who's playing.

Advertisers are attracted to this large audience and spend as much as $2.8 million for 30 seconds of airtime. That $2.8 million does not include the money that is spent actually producing the commercials, many of which are highly entertaining. In fact, polls tell us that as many as 36 percent of the people who watch do so solely for the expensive and entertaining commercials that debut during the game.

Consider the following questions. Write your response in the space provided. Use another sheet of paper, if necessary.

1. List and describe three reasons why people watch the Super Bowl. If you've ever watched all or part of a Super Bowl, are any of these reasons why you watched? Explain.

2. The day after a Super Bowl, have you talked with your friends about the game or about the advertisements during the game? If so, what did you talk about? If you did not talk about the game or had not watched the game, did you feel left out? Explain.

3. Do you ever watch a television program because you know a lot of your friends watch it? Why or why not?

A Word from Our Sponsor - - - - - - - - - - - - - - - - - - -

PROFESSIONAL AND COLLEGE SPORTS both rely heavily on marketing agreements with corporate sponsors. This may include selling the naming rights to an arena or a stadium to an advertiser, such as the Staples Center in Los Angeles, where the Lakers, Clippers, and Kings play, or FedEx Field, where the Washington Redskins play.

Spend a few minutes watching a team sports event on television, such as football or basketball, with the sound turned down.

Consider the following questions. Write your response in the space provided. Use another sheet of paper, if necessary.

1. How many advertisements do you see in the arena or stadium?

2. How many fans do you see wearing clothing with the teams' colors and logos (symbols) on them?

3. How many commercials during the game feature athletes promoting the products advertised?

4. Why do you think advertisers find sporting events such an important way of promoting their products?

Athletes: The Rich and the Famous - - - - - - - - - - - - - -

CONSIDER THE FOLLOWING QUESTIONS. Write your response in the space provided. Use another sheet of paper, if necessary.

1. In the first column of the chart below, list up to ten famous athletes whom you admire. Use the second column of the chart to write a short explanation of why you respect each person.

Name	Why you admire this person
1.	
2.	
3.	
4.	
5.	
6.	
7.	
8.	
9.	
10.	

2. Why are there so many famous athletes?

3. Why do you think so many professional athletes are paid millions of dollars each year?

You probably know that many athletes appear in advertisements for various products and services. This is called a product endorsement. The athlete demonstrates his or her support for that product or service. For example, football player LaDainian Tomlinson has appeared in Chunky Soup advertisements, basketball player LeBron James appears in Nike advertisements, and tennis player Venus Williams has appeared in advertisements for American Express. In fact, many of the more famous athletes make much more money from product endorsements than they do from playing sports. (For example, golfer Michelle Wie earned almost $20 million from product endorsements in 2007, but made less than $1 million playing golf that year.)

4. Do you know who Tiger Woods is? If so, list the name of a product that Woods endorses.

5. Do you know who Peyton Manning is? If so, list the name of a product that Manning endorses.

6. Why do advertisers want some athletes to become identified as celebrities by the public?

7. Why do advertisers pay athletes millions of dollars to endorse their products?

8. Who ultimately ends up paying for this advertising? Explain how.

9. Have you ever wanted to try a product because a famous athlete appeared in an advertisement for that product? Why or why not?

The objectives of this unit are to help students:

- understand the processes by which fame and celebrity are created

- evaluate the consequences of "extreme" television programs

- understand what empathy is and apply empathetic thinking as they watch television

- understand the role of television in the conflict between society's interests and individual rights

THE RECENT POPULARITY of reality programming offers students the chance to examine some interesting aspects of contemporary American culture. These include the willingness of many Americans to do almost anything for their "15 minutes of fame." Feeding the desire to attain fame is the public's attraction to famous people, irrespective of the source of that fame. In a society that endures a constant media barrage, the resulting desensitization of audiences compels creators of television programming to constantly "up the ante." Many shows strive to be more shocking and more titillating than they or their competitors have been previously. In this unit, students investigate the consequences of this phenomenon.

In This Unit

What Is a Celebrity? has students provide a definition for *celebrity,* identify celebrities, and explain the public's attraction to famous people.

What Price Fame? asks students to evaluate the intentional embarrassment of people on "shock talk" programs, using the notion of empathy.

What Is Real? looks at the recent trend in "reality" programming and asks students to evaluate the recent popularity of this type of programming.

Reality Shows and Social Comparison introduces students to Leon Festinger's Social Comparison Theory. Students then decide if this theory supports the popularity of reality shows and assess whether viewers benefit from watching reality shows.

Stimulus Addiction has students consider the consequences of programs that increasingly challenge social proscriptions against violence, conflict, and poor taste.

Executions on Television asks students to weigh the pros and cons of broadcasting the execution of criminals.

Cops and Cameras has students evaluate the conflict between the public's right to know and the individual's right to privacy.

Cops, Cameras, and Your Community has students appraise the positive and negative reactions to the taping of reality-based crime shows in one's community.

The Makeover asks students to judge the commercial agenda behind, and the efficacy of, this popular form of reality program.

IN THIS UNIT, WE DISCUSS programs in which the people on the programs are (supposedly) playing only themselves. The word *supposedly* is added because there are many people who speculate that at least some of the participants on these types of programs are actually paid actors, and that the producers of the programs script much of the programs' activities in advance.

Famous or Infamous?

This unit also investigates our fascination with fame—many Americans admire famous people, and many people really want to become famous themselves. Often, members of American society ignore how and why a person became famous, and focus instead on fame itself as the desired objective.

Some reality shows do indeed require participants to demonstrate some talent, such as *American Idol.* However, many reality programs feature so-called "nobodies"—ordinary people who lack significant athletic or artistic talent, and yet become famous nevertheless. These reality programs may be games of competition to avoid elimination, such as *Survivor.* Others focus on dating, marriage, or relationships, such as *Wife Swap* and *The Bachelor.* Sometimes, the people on these shows become famous for something good they have done, but others become famous for something embarrassing or even wrong. For various reasons, television viewers like to watch contestants succeed on reality programs, while viewers also like to watch other contestants fail.

What Is a Celebrity? -

ON MANY TALK SHOWS, such as *The Oprah Winfrey Show, The Ellen DeGeneres Show,* and *The Late Show with David Letterman,* people whom we refer to as "celebrities" appear and talk about what they are doing in their lives. The hosts of these programs often ask these celebrities for their opinions on things, about their reactions to current events, and often about their personal lives as well. We know that many people like to watch and listen to these celebrities, because many of these talk shows enjoy high viewership ratings.

Consider the following questions. Write your response in the space provided. Use another sheet of paper, if necessary.

1. What is your definition of a celebrity?

2. List and describe at least three characteristics of a celebrity.

3. Do all celebrities share the same characteristics, or do some celebrities have different types of characteristics from others? Explain.

4. List three people whom you consider to be celebrities. For each person, describe why that person is a celebrity.

Name of celebrity	Reasons he or she is a celebrity

5. What must a person do, or what characteristics must a person possess, to become famous?

6. Would you like to become famous? Why or why not?

7. What are some of the advantages of being famous? Explain.

8. What are some of the disadvantages of being famous? Explain.

9. Not all famous people are rich. List at least three famous people who are not rich. How did these people become famous?

10. Not all famous people are well liked. List at least three famous people who are not well liked. How did these people become famous?

What Price Fame? -

ON PROGRAMS THAT HAVE BEEN CALLED "shock talk" shows, such as *The Jerry Springer Show,* supposedly "real" people (rather than actors playing fictional characters) appear and often purposely do embarrassing things, or let other people do embarrassing things to them.

Consider the following questions. Write your response in the space provided. Use another sheet of paper, if necessary.

1. Would you be willing to do something humiliating on national television if you knew lots of people were watching? If so, what would you do?

2. Why would you or wouldn't you do something humiliating on television? Would it make a difference if you were paid to do it? Why or why not?

3. Some episodes of *American Idol* feature people who are pretty bad singers. The judges are quick to tell these people how badly they sing. Let's presume that you cannot sing very well. If you knew you were a really, really awful singer, but were offered the chance to appear on *American Idol,* would you agree to go on the show? Explain.

4. Jerry Springer once had a guest on his show who intentionally vomited during the program. On *Dr. Phil,* people are often shown as abusive spouses or parents. Why do you think people like to watch shows like Dr. Phil's and Jerry Springer's, shows where people often do or experience embarrassing things?

Empathy is the ability to identify with the way another person is feeling. To have empathy (to be empathetic), you do not have to actually experience what another person is experiencing. Instead, you can imagine yourself in the other person's situation and how you would feel if that person was you. A person can be empathetic about good things (getting a raise at work, going on a date with someone really exciting) or bad things (losing something important, getting hurt). Think about what empathy means when answering the following questions.

5. When "real" people (as opposed to actors and actresses playing characters) are embarrassed on television, do you feel embarrassed for them, or not? Explain why you feel the way you do.

6. Are your feelings about a person on television different when that person does something embarrassing on purpose, as opposed to when a person makes an embarrassing mistake? Explain.

7. Why do people like to watch shows on which other people are embarrassed? Explain.

What Is Real? -

IN THE PAST FEW YEARS, so-called "reality programs" have proven to be very popular television shows. Examples include *The Apprentice, Survivor, Fear Factor,* and *The Amazing Race.*

One of the criticisms of these shows is that much of the "reality" is actually scripted or staged. In other words, some of the things that happen on the show occur because the people making the show have told the people on the show to do or say something, or to not do or say something. There have even been claims that some of the "real" people on *The Real World* were actually professional actors.

Consider the following questions. Write your response in the space provided. Use another sheet of paper, if necessary.

1. Why does the fact that these shows are supposedly about real people in supposedly real situations make them so popular?

2. Why does it bother people to think that some of the "real" events are actually scripted or staged?

Watch one of the current reality shows.

3. What general characteristics do you think the producers of the show were looking for when they chose the participants?

4. Write down something that occurred on the show that does not seem realistic to you. Why do you think it was not realistic?

5. When we know we are being watched, most of us behave differently than we normally would. This is probably especially the case when one knows that millions of people are watching. How do you think this affects the "reality" of reality programs?

Reality Shows and Social Comparison - - - - - - - - - - - -

PSYCHOLOGIST LEON FESTINGER IDENTIFIED what he called Social Comparison Theory. Festinger said that people who are uncertain about their own abilities and attitudes will look at other people. When looking at others, people compare themselves. Festinger said that some people do this consciously at times, while at other times, they do it unconsciously. Applying this to television viewing, viewers may watch television shows to see a positive role model (attractive, hardworking, or talented) for improving himself or herself. Festinger called this upward comparison. On the other hand, viewers may watch television to observe people who they believe are lesser people than themselves (ugly, lazy, dumb, or untalented) to feel better about their own situation in life. This is what Festinger called downward comparison.

Consider the following questions. Write your response in the space provided. Use another sheet of paper, if necessary.

1. Does Festinger's Social Comparison Theory help to explain the tremendous success of reality-based programs? Explain.

2. Festinger said that when comparing ourselves to others, we normally begin with people whom we see as somewhat similar to ourselves. Is it easier for viewers to compare themselves to people on reality shows who are not (yet) famous than it is for viewers to compare themselves to actors and other celebrities who already are famous? Explain.

3. Suppose that Festinger's Social Comparison Theory is true. Do you believe that most people who watch reality programs generally benefit from watching those programs? Or can these reality programs cause unreasonable expectations among most viewers? Explain.

Stimulus Addiction -

RECENTLY, THERE HAS BEEN scientific research done on the effect of violent video games. One of the theories being discussed in this research is that if a person is routinely exposed to violence, it takes increasingly more violence to keep that person interested. The result has been labeled "stimulus addiction."

This activity applies the idea of stimulus addiction to television. Think about how reality programs such as *Survivor* and talk shows such as Jerry Springer's try to get us to watch them. These shows try to show things that are more "extreme" than usual, more extreme than whatever these shows have already done before. Of course, after a while, this becomes difficult. If something really extreme happened on a program yesterday or last week, it is quite hard to come up with a new situation that is even more extreme (especially without people getting seriously hurt or even killed).

Consider the following questions. Write your response in the space provided. Use another sheet of paper, if necessary.

1. On some of these shows, people have eaten disgusting things. Why do people want to watch this? Do you like to watch this? Why or why not?

2. On some of these shows, people have had terrible conflicts about their relationships. Often, these people end up screaming at each other, threatening each other, and trying to physically hurt each other. Why do people want to watch this? Do you like to watch this? Why or why not?

3. On some of the reality shows, people have to do things that are really difficult, really uncomfortable, or even really dangerous. Examples include walking through a snake-infested swamp or skydiving. Why do people want to watch this? Do you like to watch this? Why or why not?

4. Do you think that you are, or could become, a victim of stimulus addiction? Explain.

Executions on Television -

ON JUNE 11, 2001, Timothy McVeigh, who was convicted of killing 168 people in the April 19, 1995, bombing of the Alfred P. Murrah Federal Building in Oklahoma City, was executed. Nineteen of the victims were children. Prior to McVeigh's execution, a poll conducted by the respected Gallup Organization found that about 23 percent of Americans polled said they would have watched his execution, had it been broadcast on television.

Consider the following questions. Write your response in the space provided. Use another sheet of paper, if necessary.

1. Some people who oppose the death penalty are in favor of showing executions on television. Why do you think this is so?

2. Some people who support the death penalty are also in favor of showing executions on television. Why do you think this is so?

There are about 304 million people in the United States. If the Gallup Organization was correct, and 23 percent of Americans did want to watch the execution, that could have possibly meant an audience of nearly 80 million people. Eighty million people is a very large audience that would be attractive to advertisers. However, advertisers are selective about what types of programs they want their products associated with.

3. Many people believe that although 23 percent of those polled said publicly that they would watch the execution, the actual percentage of the population who would watch would be much higher. Why do you think this is so?

4. Osama bin Laden is believed to be the leader of the group that caused the tragedies of September 11, 2001 (9/11). Suppose the U.S. military finally captures bin Laden. Suppose further that bin Laden is tried for terrorism, is found guilty, and receives the death penalty. Do you think that bin Laden's execution should be shown on television? Explain.

5. Would you watch the execution of bin Laden? Explain.

Cops and Cameras -

ALTHOUGH THE UNITED STATES CONSTITUTION does not specifically say that citizens have a right to privacy, courts have interpreted that right as being constitutionally protected. The courts point to the First Amendment's freedom of association (our decision about whom we want to spend time with and what we do with other people) as a protection of privacy. Courts also refer to the Fourth Amendment's freedom against unreasonable searches by government agents. The Fourth Amendment says that the police usually need very good reasons to come into our homes without our permission. In addition to these constitutional protections against the government interfering with our privacy, we also have the legal right to sue private citizens who invade our privacy.

The case of Hanlon versus Berger

A number of years ago, government agents received a warrant to search a ranch in Montana. The owners of the ranch, Paul and Emma Berger, supposedly had been killing eagles, in violation of wildlife protection laws. Berger was thought to be poisoning the eagles to protect his herd of sheep. When the agents raided the ranch, they brought along a crew of camerapeople and reporters from CNN. CNN wanted to film the search of the ranch for its program *Earth Matters*. When government agents presented the warrant to the Bergers, the Bergers did not know that the agents were secretly wearing CNN microphones. Three CNN reporters searched the 75,000-acre ranch with the government agents.

No dead eagles were found. Paul Berger was convicted of illegally lacing some sheep carcasses with poison, for which he paid a $1,000 fine. CNN showed a 12-minute tape of the raid on national television.

The Bergers then filed a lawsuit, saying that the government agents and CNN had violated their right against an unreasonable search and seizure. The Bergers pointed out that CNN's participation was not mentioned in the warrant issued by a federal magistrate. The Bergers asked the courts to prohibit CNN from ever rebroadcasting the raid on television. CNN and two dozen other news agencies argued that the public's right to know, and the company's freedom of speech protection, allowed CNN to enter the ranch and to later broadcast the raid.

The United States Supreme Court decided to hear the case and ruled in the Bergers' favor.

This is an issue with competing viewpoints. Television journalists argue in favor of the public's right to know what is happening in our communities. Other people argue in favor of individuals' right to privacy.

Consider the following questions. Write your response in the space provided. Use another sheet of paper, if necessary.

1. Recall that no illegally killed eagles were found on the Bergers' ranch. Explain why you think that the Bergers were so upset at CNN.

2. Imagine that you were in the Bergers' situation, and that no killed eagles were found. Would you be upset, too? Explain.

3. There are several television programs, such as *COPS,* on which television camera teams ride with police officers. Should suspected criminals have a right to privacy that protects them from television crews entering their homes? Explain why or why not.

4. Should it make a difference whether the people whose home is searched are later found innocent, or if they are found guilty? Why or why not? Explain.

5. Explain how you would feel if the police and a television news team raided your home tonight.

6. Let's say that you are not at home, but in a public place, such as on a sidewalk or at a public park. Even though you're doing nothing wrong, this public place has a reputation for illegal activity. A camera crew from a show such as COPS walks up to you and starts taping you without your permission. Later, they show the tape of you on television. Would this bother you? Why or why not?

7. When reality-based crime television programs show real teenagers (as opposed to teenaged actors), what is usually the context? In other words, why do "real" crime programs often show teenagers? Explain.

How does this make you feel?

Cops, Cameras, and Your Community - - - - - - - - - - - -

MUCH OF A POLICE OFFICER'S JOB is quite boring. Giving traffic tickets for speeding and responding to complaints about barking dogs are not the types of police responsibilities that are likely to attract television viewers' interest. Neither is watching police officers fill out the various reports that they must file as part of their jobs. Thus, when the camera crews of television shows such as *COPS* ride along with police officers, many hours, even days, are spent waiting for exciting situations to develop.

Consider the following questions. Write your response in the space provided. Use another sheet of paper, if necessary.

1. Most people tend to overestimate how much crime really occurs in their communities. How do shows such as *COPS* cause television viewers to exaggerate the amount of crime that really occurs in their communities? Explain.

2. Do you think that reality-based crime programs make viewers more afraid of personally being victims of crime or less afraid? Explain.

Community leaders (such as the mayor, city/town manager, or chief of police) in communities where shows such as *COPS* are produced must give their consent to that taping. Some people believe that it is in a community's best interest not to allow taping of reality-based crime shows in their community. Other people support the taping of reality-based crime shows in their community.

3. Why do you think some people are against the taping of reality-based crime shows in their community? Explain.

4. Why do you think some people are in favor of the taping of reality-based crime shows in their community? Explain.

5. Would you support or oppose the taping of crime shows in your community? Explain.

The Makeover -

YOU ARE PROBABLY FAMILIAR with some of the many makeover programs that have been popular over the past few years. These include *Extreme Makeover* and *Extreme Makeover Home Edition, What Not to Wear,* and *The Biggest Loser.* Makeovers are also common features on talk shows such as *The Oprah Winfrey Show.*

The popularity of makeover shows has created a debate among different groups of people. Some people believe that makeover shows are very attractive to advertisers. They say this because makeover programs typically encourage people to spend money on various goods or services. Appearance makeover shows encourage the use of cosmetics, hair styling, clothing, gyms, spas, and even plastic surgery. Home makeover shows encourage people to spend money on home improvement and gardening products and services. Some people criticize this type of encouragement and say that people should be more willing to be happy with what they already have in life. They say that happiness cannot be bought, even though advertisers try to make it seem as if it can.

Other people say that reality for many people is unhappy. These people say that if someone has the ability to change himself or herself in order to become happier, that person should at least try, even if that requires expensive purchases.

Consider the following questions. Write your response in the space provided. Use another sheet of paper, if necessary.

1. Which side of the debate do you tend to agree with the most? Explain.

2. What is the best argument for the other side of the debate? Explain.

Although it may not be obvious at first, *Dr. Phil* is a type of makeover program. People come onto the show with some sort of emotional or personality problem, and Dr. Phil then tries to help them change. Some people believe that a person can at least begin to successfully change emotional or personality issues after talking with a trained psychologist such as Dr. Phil. Other people say that this cannot begin to happen in just an hour.

3. What's your opinion? Can meeting with somebody such as Dr. Phil for an hour help a person to remake their emotions or personality? Explain why or why not.

4. Many people are ashamed to talk to a psychologist or other personal counselor about their problems. Do you think *Dr. Phil* has made it more acceptable for people to seek psychological counseling? Explain.

Suppose that you were offered a chance to appear on a makeover show in which experts will discuss your body type, your hairstyle, and your clothing.

5. Would you be willing to appear on this show? Explain.

Glossary

advertising revenue—the money that television broadcasters make from selling advertising time during their programs. This money is the primary source of income for television broadcasters.

affiliate—a local television station that has a contract with one of the major networks, such as CBS, NBC, or ABC. Local affiliates broadcast the network's programming, in addition to their own programs. Television stations have *call letters* assigned by the federal government (see below).

call letters—the four (sometimes three) letters assigned by the Federal Communications Commission to identify a particular broadcast television station. Most stations east of the Mississippi River begin with the letter *W* (for example, WGBH in Boston). Most stations west of the Mississippi River begin with the letter *K* (for example, KTLA in Los Angeles).

conflict resolution—the way in which two or more people resolve their disputes. This can be done through negotiation and compromise, or through the use of one or more types of violence.

conglomerate—a large business corporation that owns a variety of different types of companies. For example, General Electric owns NBC, Universal Pictures, and Bravo, as well as amusement parks, medical equipment manufacturers, and financial firms.

demographics—statistics about people grouped by such information as age, gender, ethnicity, geography, and income. For example, we know that the demographic group that watches the most television is women older than 60 years of age.

Federal Communications Commission (FCC)—founded by the U.S. government in 1934, this agency is in charge of granting licenses to owners of broadcast television and radio stations, and can fine television stations that violate FCC regulations. For example, the FCC has fined Howard Stern's show several times for airing obscene material.

file footage—video recorded for earlier newscasts about the same or a similar subject; may be several days to several years old. For example, a sports story aired during the summer about a certain basketball player may use file footage of that player taped during the previous season.

gratuitous violence—violence that serves no purpose for a story's plot—it is simply included in a television show for the sake of violence itself. It is the opposite of *purposeful violence* (see next page).

narrative structure—the way a television program tells its story. Sometimes the narrative structure is linear—it has a beginning, middle, and end. Sometimes the narrative structure is nonlinear—the story is told out of the order in which depicted events occur, or several different stories are told at once. An example of a nonlinear narrative structure is a repertory drama, such as *Lost,* in which several stories are told on the same show, with the viewer being taken back and forth between different stories and even time periods.

narrowcasting—the efforts by television outlets to reach a specific demographic or psychographic group. For example, the audience for televised golf tournaments is fairly small, but attractive to certain advertisers, such as investment firms.

Nielsen rating—measurement of the United States audience for certain shows conducted by Nielsen Media Research. These ratings measure the total number of all U.S. households watching a particular program. Each rating point equals approximately 1.1 million households, or 1 percent of the estimated 110 million American households.

Nielsen share—the proportion of households using television at a particular time that are tuned to a particular program. For example, if a show had a Nielsen share of 20, that means that 20 percent of all the households that were watching television at that particular time were tuned to that particular program.

psychographics—statistics about people grouped by their interests, attitudes, values, and habits (including buying habits)

purposeful violence—violence that serves a role in a story's plot. For example, violence may be used by a heroic character to save people from a villain. It is the opposite of *gratuitous* violence (see previous page).

screen graphics—the words and other images that television broadcasters place on the screen. Screen graphics are common in sports events (scores, statistics) and news coverage (identifying people being shown, providing the location of a scene). Some screen graphics may be more dramatic than informational.

synergy—coordinated interaction between two or more organizations, designed to create a combined effect that is greater than the results those organizations could have each had on its own. For example, if McDonald's has a special toy in its kids' meals that promotes a new Disney movie, both Disney and McDonald's will make more money.

talking head—a slang expression for a television news anchorperson. The expression comes from the fact that we see little on the screen except the anchorperson's head as he or she reads the news to us.

target market—the *demographic* or *psychographic* group (see previous definitions) that the producers of a television show and its advertising sponsors want to reach. For example, a shaving cream company may want male viewers to see its advertisements, so it advertises during football games, when men are most likely to be the audience.

telegenic—somebody or something that provides a good visual image on the television screen. A person who appears very handsome or very beautiful on television would be considered telegenic. Football games are telegenic because the players wear bright uniforms, the football can be easily seen, and the playing field is an appropriate size.

uplink truck—the truck used by a television news crew doing reporting away from the studio. This truck has a satellite dish that allows it to send information up to a satellite, from which the people at the studio will download the information electronically.

Additional Resources

Publications

Bianculli, David. *Teleliteracy: Taking Television Seriously.* Syracuse: Syracuse University Press, 2000.

Carroll, Jamuna, ed. *Television: Opposing Viewpoints.* Farmington Hills, MI: Thomson Gale, 2006.

Christakis, Dimitri A., and Frederick J. Zimmerman. *The Elephant in the Living Room: Making Television Work for Your Kids.* New York: Rodale, 2006.

Crisell, Andrew. *A Study of Modern Television: Thinking Inside the Box.* New York: Palgrave Macmillan, 2006.

Edgerton, Gary R. *The Columbia History of American Television.* New York: Columbia, 2007.

Fox, Roy F. *Harvesting Minds: How TV Commercials Control Kids.* Westport, CT: Praeger, 2000.

Heller, Dana. *Makeover Television: Realities Remodeled.* New York: Taurus, 2007.

Huff, Richard M. *Reality Television.* Westport, CT: Praeger, 2006.

Lemish, Dafna. *Children and Television: A Global Perspective.* Malden, MA: Blackwell, 2007.

Lotz, Amanda. *The Television Will Be Revolutionized.* New York: New York University, 2007.

Newcomb, Horace, ed. *Television: The Critical View.* 7th ed. New York: Oxford, 2006.

Potter, W. James. *Media Literacy.* 4th ed. Thousand Oaks, CA: Sage, 2008.

Ross, Sharon Marie, and Louisa Stein, eds. *Teen Television: Essays on Programming and Fandom.* Jefferson, NC: McFarland, 2008.

Web Sites

Center for Media Literacy
www.medialit.org

Center for Social Media
www.centerforsocialmedia.org

Children Now: Media
www.childrennow.org/issues/media

Media Awareness Network
www.media-awareness.ca

Media Literacy Online Project
interact.uoregon.edu/medialit/mlr/home

National Association for Media Literacy Education
www.namle.net

New Mexico Media Literacy Project
www.nmmlp.org/index.html

Nielsen Media Research
www.nielsenmedia.com

PBS Parents—TV Viewer's Guide: Teens
www.pbs.org/parents/childrenandmedia/tvviewersguide-teens.html

extending and enhancing learning

Let's stay in touch!

Thank you for purchasing these Walch Education materials. Now, we'd like to support you in your role as an educator. **Register now** and we'll provide you with updates on related publications, online resources, and more. You can register online at www.walch.com/newsletter, or fill out this form and fax or mail it to us.

Name _____ Date _____

School name _____

School address_____

City _____ State _____ Zip _____

Phone number (home) _____ (school) _____

E-mail _____

Grade level(s) taught _____ Subject area(s) _____

Where did you purchase this publication? _____

When do you primarily purchase supplemental materials? _____

What moneys were used to purchase this publication?

[   ] School supplemental budget

[   ] Federal/state funding

[   ] Personal

[   ] Please sign me up for Walch Education's free quarterly e-newsletter, *Education Connection.*

[   ] Please notify me regarding free *Teachable Moments* downloads.

[   ] Yes, you may use my comments in upcoming communications.

COMMENTS _____

_____

_____

_____

Please FAX this completed form to 888-991-5755, or mail it to:
Customer Service, Walch Education, 40 Walch Drive, Portland, ME 04103